The Patchwork Of My Life

Memoirs of the Wife of a POW

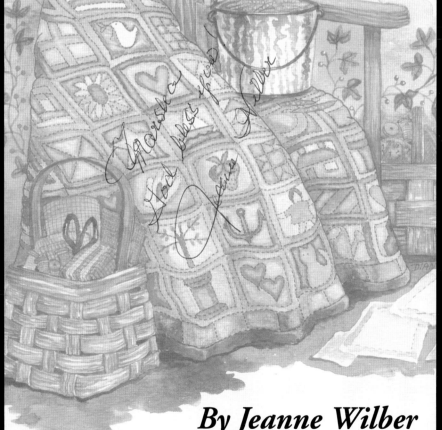

By Jeanne Wilber

About the Cover

The artist and dear friend is Diane Knott from Mansfield, Pennsylvania – Chicken Scratch Designs. For years I sold her and husband Mickey's products – Knott's in Wood – in my shop but it was never a "business deal." When they first moved to this area they came to visit The Strawberry Patch and it was love at first sight! – we talked for an hour. God has blessed us with a beautiful friendship.

This is Diane's description of the cover picture:

"I used the following images on the quilt: Flag, boat, star and anchor to show Gene's military life, the cross, heart-in-hand and dove for your faith in God, the strawberry and spool of thread for The Strawberry Patch, all the hearts are for your marriage and the love you all have for EVERYONE,

houses and log cabin patch for your home, sunflower and watering can for your love of gardening, the tree is your family tree with you and Gene being the top two branches and the other four your children, the Ohio star patch because you once told me it was your favorite . . . the bucket of peas and hand shovel on the quilt are pretty self explanatory (smile), and the patches on the ground are the unfinished chapters of your life . . .

Page Icon by Diane Knott

Dear Lord,
I hope with all
my ♥ that there
will be quilting
in heaven . . .

Dedication

This book is dedicated to my Grandchildren: John, Joe, Summer (& Mat), Matthew, Chris, Andrew, Mattea, Isaac, Maryah, Mishala, Rachael, Daniel, Anna, Mikaela, Abram, Miina; and my Great grandchildren: Cole, Luke and all who will follow. You were my inspiration and reason for wanting to put my thoughts down on paper in order that you would know how your Grandma thinks. I didn't write much about you because the book is for you. It would have made interesting reading to write a chapter about each of you because your lives are unique and beautiful but the intent of the book is for you to know more about your parents and grandparents and the roots we have established for you. If the book gives you a desire to keep the roots nourished and help each other grow to serve God and do some good in the world then it will have served its purpose. We want the very best for you and that will surely come as you carry on this simple faith and remain engulfed in His abiding love.

When I read your great, great Grandmother's diaries I felt as if I really knew her and I hope my writing will help you understand me better. We often eat together, talk to each other, sit around a campfire, pick stones from the garden, weed, catch bugs, shell peas, snip beans, husk corn, make horseradish, pick berries or crabapples, crack nuts by the fireplace, put puzzles together and do so many things; but we don't always take enough time to get into each other's heart and that is why I am opening my heart for you to get a glimpse of what is inside me. I love you dearly and I treasure our times together. I pray for each of you by name every day and I will continue to do that. I do hope you enjoy this little journey into the heart and life of your Grandma.

RCW Publishing Company
presents
The Patchwork of My Life
Memoirs of the Wife of a POW
©2001 by Jeanne Wilber

Rebecca C. Wilber Publishing Company
The Inn at Old Post Lane
RR#3, Box 43, Columbia Cross Roads, Pennsylvania 16914-9535
800-333-4RCW International calls: 570-549-3331 fax: 570-549-3332
www.rcwpublishing.com email rcw@epix.net

ISBN 1-889825-07-7

TABLE of CONTENTS

Take My Life and Let It Be

HENDON

FRANCES R. HAVERGAL, 1836-1879   H. A. César Malan, 1787-1864

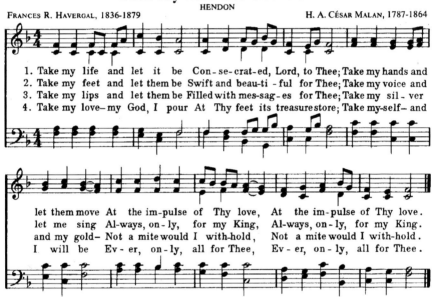

1. Take my life and let it be Con-se-crat-ed, Lord, to Thee; Take my hands and
2. Take my feet and let them be Swift and beau-ti-ful for Thee; Take my voice and
3. Take my lips and let them be Filled with mes-sag-es for Thee; Take my sil-ver
4. Take my love—my God, I pour At Thy feet its treasure store; Take my-self— and

let them move At the im-pulse of Thy love, At the im-pulse of Thy love.
let me sing Al-ways, on-ly, for my King, Al-ways, on-ly, for my King.
and my gold— Not a mite would I with-hold, Not a mite would I with-hold.
I will be Ev-er, on-ly, all for Thee, Ev-er, on-ly, all for Thee.

6

PART ONE

Take My Life and Let It Be

It was exactly midnight, Father's Day, 1968, when the doorbell rang. Mom and I were still up - just talking to each other in the living room of her home in northern Pennsylvania. We had been having some late nights because my Dad had died eleven days earlier and this seemed to be the most difficult time of day for her. It was encouraging to see that she was beginning to look forward to our time together after my four children were sound asleep upstairs in their beds. My husband, Gene, was a Navy pilot on the aircraft carrier USS America off the coast of Vietnam.

It seemed an unusual time for anyone to call - that is why I checked my watch and saw that the hands were tight together at midnight.

Still wanting to protect Mom from unnecessary encounters - I went to the door expecting to see a friendly neighbor from down the country road who saw our lights and not being able to sleep either, was stopping in for coffee or tea and conversation - or perhaps it was someone in distress. The last thing I anticipated was what I saw.

Before opening the kitchen door I turned on the porch light. At that point it seemed everything started happening in slow motion. My heart beat like a hammer against my ribs. Each thud reminded me of a camera shutter methodically snapping pictures that would stay in my mind's eye forever. Two uniformed men stood on the porch. As I opened the door for them they asked if I was Mrs. Wilber, but before they asked I knew their mission. They stepped inside and told me that my dear husband Gene was Missing in Action.

Could this be real? Whatever happened to the carefree days?

7

Chapter One

"I've Found a Friend"

I grew up in a happy home with a loving Mom and Dad. When I was ten my only brother, Jim, was born.

By the time I was thirteen we had lived in ten different places so it was good to settle down and establish roots on a farm between Daggett and Jobs Corners, PA. That turned out to be the most eventful summer of my young life - I met the two people that would change my life forever.

My family and I were visiting my Aunt, Uncle and three cousins in Roulette, PA. On Sunday evening we attended the service in their little church. Aunt Marguerite was the church pianist and a Sunday School teacher so I always enjoyed going there. On this particular Sunday evening, my cousin Shirley and I sat in front of my Mom and Dad. Have you ever been struck with an uncontrollable fit of laughter? Why does it always happen in a quiet place and why is it so much more prevalent among young teenage girls? Shirley and I didn't plan it and we struggled to be sober but everything struck us funny - even thinking about sad things (like how much trouble we were making for ourselves) made us want to roll on the floor. We tried our best to demonstrate self-control and suppress the ugly snorts that were coming from deep within us - trying to burst out of our throats and noses. Our bodies shook, we thought our sides would split open and tears were pouring down our cheeks.

How could Jesus want a girl like that? As quickly as the fit came - it left - and I starting hearing a message I had never heard before - one about personal commitment. I couldn't stop listening and I was overwhelmed to learn of God's

great love for me. All my life I had prayed "Now I lay me down to sleep...." at bedtime but I never realized that I had to open my heart's door to let Him in for it to really work.

Before long the minister was giving an invitation and this was another hurdle for me to climb. I was an obedient daughter and I loved my mother very much but I knew she didn't approve of my Aunt's church. Not wanting to displease her, I kept my hand at my side. With my head bowed I began to think of how much I loved Jesus and I knew I wanted Him in my heart forever. My arm seemed weightless - it was as if Someone had tied a string around my wrist and pulled it up toward heaven - so there I stood with my hand held high in the air. That was the beginning of my life!

Outside the church Mom was silent when I embraced her but I'll never forget Aunt Marguerite's warm, fat hug and her tear brimmed eyes.

Little did I know when I met Gene Wilber that summer of 1943 that he would be my best friend for ten years and then the love of my life forever. Gene and I were in the same class at Troy High School. I couldn't date until I was eighteen and by then Gene had joined the Navy and I entered Mansfield College to prepare to be a music teacher. Every time he came home on leave it seemed I was away but he always had a good visit with my parents.

Through my college years I prayed for and about the man I would marry - I wanted "a marriage made in heaven" - one that God had planned and I kept asking Him to make me know for sure when the right one came along. I met many outstanding young men while I was in college and had lots of friends but no one ever compared with Gene Wilber. I always thought about him and kept his picture in my room. He came home for Christmas when I was in my second year of college and then we didn't see each other again for 3-1/2 years. Gene never told me he cared for me and he was too busy to write. I was just proper enough that I would have never expressed my feelings first.

My first teaching job was in Addison, NY and I loved it. In the spring of that year I was offered a job in Elmira,

NY to supervise music in three schools. It was a good pay raise and the nice part was being able to live at home (only a thirteen mile drive) so I accepted.

One evening that summer Mom and I were sorting buttons at a card table in the den. Dad and Jim were reading. Someone knocked at the kitchen door and since I was sitting on the sofa where it was hard to get out - Mom went to the door. When I heard her say "Why, Gene Wilber!" my heart nearly stopped and all the dreams I had about our meeting again went out the window.

Even a twenty-three-year-old music teacher who still lives at home with her Mom, Dad and little brother spends time imagining romantic scenarios about the young man that has captured her heart without his even knowing it. I drove to Elmira frequently and passed his Mother and Dad's home on the way; there was always the hope that his car would be there. When I walked down our dirt road to the creek, I'd wish he would be leaning against the bridge - waiting for me to skip stones on the water as we had when we were kids. I always hoped to see him "across a crowded room" as the popular song suggested. Even when I was shopping, I'd dream of rushing around a busy corner and falling into his arms - -

But those are dreams

And this is reality -

When Mom yelled I jumped up and spilled the whole card table. Buttons went flying and I had my head under the sofa with rear end up when he walked into the room. I was on my feet in a minute and even with my hair askew and my cheeks beet red he could still smile at me. Oh! - it was so good to see him again!

After we all picked up buttons, the five of us sat down to visit. Gene had just returned from Korea so he had much to tell us about his life aboard an aircraft carrier and his experiences as a night attack pilot were very fascinating. It was hard to imagine him finding the aircraft carrier at night out in the ocean and landing a plane on it while it was pitching with the waves.

Jim went to bed at his regular time. Normally I was the next to go - around 9:30. Mom and Dad always stayed

up late. I couldn't believe my eyes on this evening - at 10:30 Dad forced a yawn and asked Mom if it wasn't past their bedtime, so upstairs they went.

Gene and I walked to the kitchen thinking it must be time for him to leave. As he walked to the door I stood across the room and told him how much we enjoyed his visit and asked him to come again during his leave time. He said he would and with his back toward me, his hand on the doorknob, he said, "You have really had me worried." And I asked "Why?" I guess he didn't realize how long I would have waited for him. God wasn't going to let me marry anyone else! He came back and put his arms around me. How good it was to have him hold me. We had much to talk about and it was then that he told me he loved me for the very first time.

His leave was up before we knew it but he hinted that we might get married early the next summer after my school year was over. It was hard to say goodbye to him. San Diego, California seemed so far away but we made plans for him to call me in Elmira at my Aunt Ruth's where I stayed every Wednesday night. I was soprano soloist at Hedding Methodist Church and had choir practice then. Calling me at home was out of the question - we had an eight-party line and everyone knew us and was as excited about our romance as our families were.

11

Chapter Two

A Marriage Made in Heaven

By October, Gene found out that he had to go back to Korea again at the end of March (he was the only Navy night attack pilot to deploy twice to Korea). He asked if we could be married during my Christmas vacation. He wanted to send my engagement ring, but I wanted to wait until he could put it on my finger. I was delighted when his commanding officer let him fly a Navy plane home for Thanksgiving. He was only home for 24 hours, but that was plenty of time to put the ring on my finger.

We were married on December 27, 1952. Gene was due home on December 23rd so we could get our marriage license. He didn't arrive. On the 24th I went to City Hall in Elmira and explained our predicament. The clerk was wonderful! She told me she would take the paper and her seal to her home and we could go there on Christmas morning. When I got home from Elmira he still wasn't home. I was getting so concerned that I was sick with worry and I had to sing at the midnight Christmas Eve service. Just as I was getting ready to leave, he walked in. What a relief!!

Gene had become a Christian when he was thirteen also - we had a strong foundation. On our wedding night we knelt down and prayed together asking the Lord to bless our marriage and hold us close together and we pledged our service to Him.

After Gene and I were married our honeymoon was a hurried five-day trip to Coronado, California. He had rented an apartment for us but it wasn't going to be available for a few days, so we went to the Hotel Del Coronado. We arrived Sunday evening and what a paradise it was. I was on the edge of my seat - not wanting to miss anything and Gene smiled at

*Even then, Gene protectively guarded our footsteps
in order that I could be freely jubilant.*

his country girl who had never seen a palm tree before. After we
checked in at the hotel, he took me to three different homes to
introduce me to the wives of his squadron teammates because he
was going to have to leave me alone for the week - he had to leave
at 5:30 the next morning.

Those three wives were such a blessing to me! They taught
me how to find my way around Coronado and the Naval Air Station at North Island. They also introduced me to other
Navy wives and took turns having me over for dinner. They
took up the slack and helped me get through my first sepa-

13

ration from Gene and also the first time away from my family in Pennsylvania.

When Gene came home on Friday afternoon, I had everything moved into our apartment. We went right out and bought groceries and we were in business! A home of our own! What a joy to cook for him, do laundry and add touches to decorate the apartment. And to see him in the chair reading the paper - my heart was so full and I loved him so much!

Was it any wonder I was smitten?

He had to leave again early Monday morning and that is the way it was - we spent seven weekends and a few workdays together before he left for Korea.

A few days before he left I went to a doctor to see why I felt so queasy. I was ecstatic to learn that I was going to have a baby and I couldn't wait to tell Gene. He was happy but concerned that he had to be gone nine months and I would have to go through it all alone. We named Bruce before he left.

It was so hard to say goodbye and it got harder as the years went by. It always felt like a portion of my heart was being torn out. Gene was such a part of me - even then when we were newlyweds.

Mother and Dad Wilber flew out to say goodbye to Gene and to help me drive back to Pennsylvania. As we traveled, I tried to be good company but I felt so sick and I cried for Gene long into each night. I was very thankful to

14

be carrying his baby and have a part of him right with me. When I prayed I could only be thankful for the way God had blessed me - He would always keep us close together...more tears...but they were grateful tears of joy.

To some it might seem that Gene and I were being separated by a huge crevasse as he traveled west to Korea and I traveled east to the hills of North central Pennsylvania but Gene was praying for me and I was praying for him and God had made us one. It was always like a triangle with God at the top reaching down to each of us and we extending that love to each other. Our daily letters and sometimes two, three or four a day kept us in tune with the events of our lives.

My family was waiting for me with open arms as were my Grandmother, aunts, uncles, cousins, Gene's family and our friends. But I was sick - yuk! Some women have no sign of morning sickness while others have it for three months. I had it all day, every day for nine months and even had to be hospitalized during my fifth month. I learned to live with it and stayed fairly active.

The bleakness of early April came to life as signs of spring brought new hope. How I love the first appearance of spring - the honking of geese as they announce their pilgrimage north to quicken the hearts and entice those of us below to look up and gaze at the wavering V that they form in the sky, the return of robins; the sound of the rushing, swollen creek as it crashes against its banks and bounds over the stones carrying the last remnants of melted snow from all the hills around us; the crocus and daffodils reaching like fingers from the soil and the rain washed freshness of green grass and flowering trees.

One morning I was sitting on the step at the end of the walk that led to our mailbox across the dirt road - just breathing in the beauty of life and the sun-drenched day. Dew drops were still on the blades of grass and the flowers around me - what peace and beauty! I heard a noise. It was a crackling sound and I thought it might be a field mouse under the decaying leaves in the flowerbed. I picked up a stick and started poking in the leaves. My face nearly touched the bud of an iris and I

15

heard the crackle again — I looked at the bud and it was opening. Spellbound I watched the whole spectacular production complete with sound effects, motion and fragrance until it presented itself in full glory to the world. How can anyone not believe in God - the Great Creator of all things when they experience something like that? If He loves and takes such special care of His flowers, surely He will love and care for us - we are His children!

Soon it was summer and then the halfway point - the countdown is much easier than the climb up! I was most fortunate to have two exciting things to look forward to - the birth of our first baby and the homecoming of my wonderful husband.

We never could decide on a girl's name. With nearly every letter during those last months, girl names would fly half way around the world and back again. It is a good thing Bruce Edgar was a boy so I could call him by name as soon as I held him in my arms on November 14, 1953. Words cannot express the incredible joy! The tears of thanksgiving! The love beyond measure! And then suddenly the realization that Gene would be home in two weeks.

I could hardly wait for Gene to see our baby boy but as the day drew closer I became concerned about my own condition - would he still love me in this shape I was in? He did! He really loved me with all his heart and Bruce was his pride and joy! Oh, dear Lord, thank You for these beautiful treasures You have given me! Thank You for hearts brimming with love. Thank You for watching over us. Thank You for enveloping us in Your arms - we are a family!

Life sped on - military life keeps you on a strict schedule but that didn't bother us since we were habitually scheduled anyway. After a few days at home we loaded our car with all our belongings and baby gear and headed for California again. We made a snug little bed on the front seat between us for Bruce. It is a good thing I nursed him - we wouldn't have had room for or the capability to make formula. Life was wonderful! We were happy and we were together!!

16

Chapter Three

Gene Came Home for Lunch

We spent four months in Coronado, then off to Kingsville, Texas with a side trip of nearly 4000 miles to Pennsylvania to let everyone see how beautiful Bruce was at five months old. Gene was a flight instructor for three years in Kingsville. What a perfect place for us to really establish ourselves as a family. We bought our first home, Gene came home for lunch, we joined a church that was just starting, I directed the choir, Gene came home for lunch, we had wonderful neighbors, our Navy friends were the best, two good friends from high school (Clyde and Ray) were stationed nearby and came weekends to work on their cars and eat home cooked food (Gene instructed Ray) and Bruce and I were content because, it was so special that Gene could come home for lunch!!

Those times that Gene came home for lunch stand out in my memory because they were a solidifying factor in our family life and we formed habits that remain to this day. Bruce could have been a marathon creeper - he performed the act with great energy, speed and style. He was very agile and you could hear him coming because he slapped the floor with flair as he moved. Occasionally he would lower his blond curly head and then lift it high in the air to show his glee, reminding us of a frisky colt. When, at lunchtime each day, he would hear our car pull into the carport, he could hardly contain himself as he sped to the kitchen screen door, pulled himself up and laughingly, pounding his palms against the screen, waited for Daddy to run up the steps, open the door and sweep him up high in the air. What joyful laughter came from both of them as Gene stood there in his uniform with our son in his arms. By the time Gene greeted me with a kiss I had our lunch on the table. When we sat down with Bruce between us he quickly outstretched both arms to hold our hands

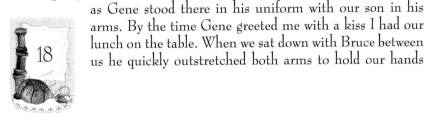

18

and we extended our free hand to each other. Before Gene and I had time to bow our heads Bruce had his face flat in his plate where it stayed until Gene finished the prayer and said "Amen." During lunch we shared the happenings of our morning with each other and then Gene played on the floor with Bruce for a few minutes before going back to work. After our kisses goodbye were ex-

Bruce with his face in the plate

changed I stood in the doorway holding Bruce and we waved until Daddy was out of sight. As soon as Bruce could talk, Gene taught him to thank me for the good meal and give me a hug. Our children still do that and I treasure their thoughtfulness, as I also treasure their Dad for instilling that quality of appreciation in them from the very beginning.

The most significant event during our years in Kingsville was the birth of our second son, Thomas Eugene.

Bruce was the love of our lives! I remember holding and rocking him when he was ten months old. I had just learned that I was going to have another baby and of course I was jubilant! But as I held Bruce in my arms I started to cry because I didn't know how I could share the love I had for him. I didn't want to take any of it away and my heart was so full of love right then I didn't know how it could hold anymore.

But God is so good! As that new baby grew inside me a new love was blooming in my heart - at that same time the special love I had for Bruce was growing.

19

Gene is a strong man - not easily drawn to tears - but on Father's Day, June 19, 1955 when our son, Thomas, was born, his shining blue eyes filled with tears that streamed freely down his cheeks. I was so thankful Gene was with me this time. It was comforting to share the joy with him.

I still remember that early morning at the Kleburg County Hospital when I first held Thomas in my arms. I remember the softness, the warmth, the sweet smell, the perfect head, the tiny chin, the closed eyes, the ever moving mouth, the tiny hand that held my finger as I tearfully thanked God for him and asked the Lord to use him in a special way. He had such a dignified look that Gene and I called him "Mister Thomas" for quite a long time.

I also thank You today, Lord for etching the treasured, joy-filled moments of our lives on the walls of our hearts so we can recall them many years later and be filled, once again, with the same outpouring of gratitude!

Thomas and Bruce in Kingsville, Texas

THE PATCHWORK of MY LIFE

Chapter Four

Blessings and Adversities

Those glorious days of togetherness came to an end when Gene received orders to catapult school at the Naval Air Facility in Philadelphia for the summer months and then on to Jacksonville, Florida in 1957. We were to be in that area for the next four years. Gene was the Catapult Officer on the aircraft carrier Essex home ported in Mayport for two years and after that he was in VF11 flying Crusaders at Cecil Field.

We bought a lovely brick home in a peaceful neighborhood. With Gene away on nine to eleven month cruises to the Mediterranean, it was a blessing to be placed in an area where neighbors became like family. We lived on the ocean side of the St. John's River - away from the city and only a ten-minute drive to the beach.

Gene worked hard as catapult officer but he loved it and built some strong friendships with fellow officers on the ship. When they were nearing the end of one of their cruises (and we were all excited to be in final count down) they were ordered to the coast of Lebanon because of the crisis there. Gene never worked as hard. At one time he worked around the clock and then only had time for an occasional catnap on the flight deck because they were launching groups of airplanes every hour and fifteen minutes for about seven days and he never had time to go to his bed. Normally there were two catapult officers but because the tour supposedly ended in the Mediterranean, the other officer was sent home. When they were in Lebanon, Gene was the only qualified catapult officer.

After the crisis in Lebanon, China was threatening Formosa (now Taiwan), so the ship went through the Suez Canal (the Essex was the first ever aircraft carrier to go through the Canal) which was the shortest route to Formosa. The ship supported U.S. policy, which was helping Formosa stand against Communist China. When they left the Pacific they went around South Africa to South America and back to Florida. It was a very long trip.

The strain of that extended tour must have been good for us because we were even closer when he returned. I'm thankful we never built up petty indifferences while we were apart and I'm thankful for the abiding trust we had in each other. We never had to make adjustments when we got back together. We always just fit! To us the abnormal times (that we had to learn to cope with) were the months of separation. The times together were too precious to hang a cloud over.

There was a bad fire on the Essex one day when they were practicing takeoffs and landings a few miles off the coast of Florida. One of Gene's shipmates called me just before the 11 o'clock news to say that he had just landed at the airfield and Gene had asked him to call me to say that he was okay. When I watched the news I was thankful Gene had gotten the message to me. The accident was horrible. A plane crashed into the ramp of the ship, exploded and caught the ship on fire. The flight deck was wooden and soaked with aviation fuel. The crashed plane careened across the flight deck striking other airplanes before it went over the side, wrecked planes full of fuel had to be untied, loosened and pushed overboard, and water was spewing from fire hoses as men worked frantically.

Because of the flames and the heavy black smoke from the burning tires, wood and fuel, the ship had to keep turning to keep the wind blowing the fire and smoke away from the island (a super structure that sticks up at the right side of the flight deck and contains the Admiral's bridge, the Captain's bridge and the air boss [control tower]). The fire fighters were dressed appropriately but most of the men up there were in summer flight deck clothing. Gene saw an enlisted man burning under a plane and pulled him out. The man's shirt was on fire so Gene removed his own shirt and used it to put the fire out. Then he covered the man with his own body until medical help arrived. Gene's chest and arms were burned.

23

A few months later Gene asked me to go with him to a ceremony aboard the Saratoga. I had no idea that Gene would be presented with the Navy Marine Medal for Heroism for his actions the day of the fire. He had neglected telling me about it. I always heard praises about Gene from his commanding officers or fellow pilots concerning his skills of flying, his work ethic, his leadership qualities and his characteristics of integrity and loyalty but I never heard any of these things from Gene - my strong yet gentle husband with the kindly smiling eyes.

When Gene's tour as catapult officer was over we moved to California for three months. He had been selected to go to the University of Southern California to study Aircraft Accident Investigation.

We found an apartment on Los Feliz Boulevard in Hollywood. The boys enjoyed it there because we had a nice pool at the apartment building and there were parks within easy walking distance. Bruce went to first grade in a nearby elementary school, Gene went to class every weekday and studied hard when he was home, Thomas and I had extra time together, which we both enjoyed. Both boys started talking early and loved to have me read to them but I was quite surprised when Thomas started reading back to me - he was only three. I thought it might be memorization but we got a new book *Jerry Learns to Button*. I read it once and he read it back. I'd point to a word out of context and he would tell me the word.

While we were there we renewed the lasting relationships that we had with Nan and Herb, friends from our Kingsville days. Herb had resigned from the Navy and was working for Lockheed. They lived in the San Fernando Valley and had a beach house at Long Beach where we enjoyed a few blissful weekends with them.

The foreboding queasiness came over me again and I became all dewy-eyed and thankful. Poor Gene - how did he put up with the mother in me? - Sick as a dog and yet happy as a lark!

Gene's classes ended and once more my pride in him escalated. He was the only non-college graduate, non-engineer to take the rigorous course and he was top student.

24

Gene had been one of the brightest students in our high school class but didn't have the opportunity to go on to college. He joined the Navy when he was eighteen and only served as an enlisted man for thirteen months. He had taken an aptitude test during boot camp at Great Lakes. I'm thankful God gave him such clear-minded thinking because he ranked very high on that test and was ordered to Pensacola for flight training. He then became an officer and was an Ensign when we married.

We were all happy to get back to our neighborhood and home in Jacksonville. Gene had a longer ride to work at Cecil Field but was eager to start flying again. Bruce enjoyed getting back in his own school where he knew all of his classmates. Thomas was perpetually happy to have his own big lawn with the playhouse Daddy had made for the boys and to have all his little friends to play with every day. I was happy to get my house back in order and make it a home again.

Gene had to leave for the Mediterranean on July 2nd (when our baby was due). My doctor was going to induce labor on June 28th but when he examined me he decided against it because I wasn't ready. My disappointment was hard to conceal because I really wanted Gene to see this baby before he left. Our second car, a little Fiat, was the most uncomfortable car to ride in. It bumped along like a little lumber wagon, so we thought it would be a good idea to go for a long drive that evening.

It worked! Mark Edward was born on June 30, 1960. How could we be so blessed? Gene and I were bursting with thanksgiving for Mark and our hearts melted when we saw how perfect, fair and beautiful he was. Such strength he had in his grip as he held onto his Daddy's little finger! Mark seemed to be intuitive right from the start to the need for him to be good and cooperative in order for us to get the "show on the road" and be back home before Daddy had to leave. I remember how thankful I was to have Gene with us but it was a very confusing time. When Mark was two days old, Gene picked us up at the hospital in the morning, took us home and settled us in. He kissed us all goodbye (a very tearful goodbye) and he left.

25

My own thanksgiving for Mark came with the joy he brought me. That joy helped absorb the sorrow of Gene's departure and the weeks to come were filled with my nurturing of him and caring for Bruce and Thomas. Gene was only gone for three months, which is hard enough to bear, but it is much better than the average cruise length of nine months.

When Gene returned in the fall it seemed we were extra busy. He had to leave again the first week of January. His workload was heavy with longer hours and added training to prepare for the cruise.

We couldn't wait for the week of leave time that Gene would have at Christmas. Joyful as you want to be, the underlying dread of separation bruises your heart whenever you think about it. You try your best to cover those feelings up to each other and to the boys, but you can't. It's in your eyes, it's in the gentle embraces, it's in the softness of your voice and it's in your tears at bedtime - your heart is already longing for what you already have.

On December 21st, Gene was working on the Fiat in the garage getting it tuned up for the months he would be gone. Bruce got his jacket on before going to the back yard to rake pine needles (which was a never-ending job for all of us since we had seventy large pine trees in our yard). I gave him an extra hug before he went out. Then I went to Mark who was in the crib - he was at that delightful age of nearly six months old.

Suddenly Gene burst into my hearing, yelling and running down the hall. I turned to see him standing in the bedroom doorway holding Bruce in his arms. I was horrified when I looked at Bruce and saw his eye out of the socket and hanging down on his chin. Gene told me that Bruce had done it with a chisel in the garage. My first reaction was to love and comfort Bruce but Gene told me to call the doctor. While I called our pediatrician, I could hear our car screeching out of the driveway. As soon as I finished the conversation I ran to the door but my heart sank to see that I had been left behind. I *had* to be with Bruce! Immediately, like an answer to prayer, my dear neighbor Phyllis hurried over and said that she would take care of Thomas and Mark and our neighbor Harold from across the street had already backed his car out of the driveway to pick me up and

follow Gene. Neither of them knew what was wrong - they just realized our distress and were there to help in anyway they could. Do you wonder I love them to this day?

We didn't catch him until we arrived at the doctor's. Gene and Bruce were in our car. The nurse had run out and put a gauze patch over Bruce's eye saying she had called the best eye surgeon in the southeast and the police would take us there. Within seconds the police car came and as he opened the door for me Gene was putting Bruce in my arms. We sped off with siren's blaring and Gene following.

The police car arrived at the Medical Center first and I jumped out with Bruce in my arms. With the policeman leading the way we ran across the lot, through the lobby, up the elevator to the seventh floor, down the hall, through Dr. Houston's waiting room and into the examining room with people holding doors open all the way. When I put Bruce on the table Gene was there beside me.

After Dr. Houston examined Bruce, he concluded that it would be best to remove the eye. When he started to tell us what wonderful things were being done with glass eyes, Gene and I both felt sick. We just didn't feel right about this. We wanted him to save the eye. He told us the lens was lost when the gauze was put over the eye.

We were hurried off to the hospital that stood within sight of the Medical Center. While Bruce was in the operating room we prayed constantly for him and for Dr. Houston. Our minister came and prayed with us also.

After the 3-1/2 hour operation, Dr. Houston came and stood in the doorway. He looked tired but calm and said, "I don't know what made me do it but I left the eye in and filled it with saline solution." He had done tedious repair work and had stitched all around the eye.

We thanked him and told him it was an answer to our prayers. Dr. Houston had a special quality: not only was he highly respected for his surgical skill, he also had a relaxed way of explaining every detail in layman's terms in order for one

27

to understand the procedure he used. We trusted his ability to take care of Bruce because his demeanor reflected love and compassion and a desire to do his best for our son. He also responded favorably to our faith in God.

The following morning the eye was still inflated and we were thankful! Bruce was finally able to tell us what had happened. He had gone to the garage to see his Dad and while Gene worked on a tire, Bruce picked up a chisel he saw lying on the workbench. He decided to carve a Christmas tree in the 2 x 4 that framed the doorway between the garage and workshop. With both hands on the chisel he placed it on the wood in front of him but when he made his first upward gouge in the wood, it slipped and went into his eye. It happened so quickly he didn't have time to blink. The 1/2" chisel went in vertically but never touched either eyelid. He used such force that the chisel went through the eye to less than 1/4" from the brain.

The day for Gene to deploy came all too quickly and needless to say, it was unusually difficult for all of us. The weeks that followed were arduous and filled with constant care for Bruce. At one point he came down with red measles that resulted in some unexpected complications. In the spring, Dr. Houston's receptionist called to tell me to listen to him on the radio the following Sunday night. I sat alone in the kitchen after the boys had gone to bed and heard Dr. Houston's voice saying "I would like to tell you about the miracle of my profession." I wept as I thanked God for all His blessings!

Thirteen years later Bruce had a cornea transplant at Wills Eye Hospital in Philadelphia, PA and after further

Thomas, Mark and Bruce in Jacksonville, Florida

28

treatment he had 20-20 vision. Now I tease him about going down-hill, as we all do. (At forty-seven, he is ready for bifocals.)

Blessings come from adversity. The weaker I felt during those days, the more I turned to my Lord and Savior. He was always there! The more I leaned on Him, the stronger I felt and I knew the strength came from Him. I often thought of the day of the accident and was thankful Gene was home and that God put the right people in the right places all along the way. I thought how blessed we are as His creations to know that He provides us with extra adrenaline to be used during crisis situations to help us think clearly, stay levelheaded and produce strength beyond our normal capacity. I was strong, healthy and active but normally it would have been strenuous work to run and carry even a twenty-five pound toddler that long distance from the police car to the examining table. Bruce, however, at seven years old was nearly half my size. I appreciated also that Thomas and Mark were never neglected - with one child convalescing, the four of us spent more time reading, playing games and just having fun. Good came out of calamity - our family was stronger, our trust more heartfelt and our faith was firm.

That summer of 1961 Gene urged me to come to Europe. His squadron had been off loaded to Rota, Spain because the aircraft carrier was crowded. He had accumulated leave time and wanted me to be with him. It was difficult for me to think of leaving the boys, but I took them home to Mom and Dad, flew to Madrid and into the loving arms of my husband. We really needed those few weeks together. One of the younger bachelors in the squadron had purchased a new Mercedes sports convertible, an SL190. When he heard I was coming, he insisted that Gene and I use it for our trip. What a glorious time we had and what a perfect time to be traveling through Europe. With the rate of exchange in our favor and hotel accommodations costing very little we were able to stay at four star Grand Hotels for only $12.00 a night. We dined and danced on rooftops, ate breakfast on the private balconies of our rooms and laughed because Gene had gone to Special Services before he left Rota, Spain and selected camping gear for us. It was neatly packed in the trunk of the car and there it stayed for the entire trip.

29

We traveled from Madrid to Bordeaux to Paris then on to Strasbourg, Stuttgart and Heidelberg, Germany, through the Black Forest to Zurich and Luzern, Switzerland, over the winding roads of the Alps to Italy where we went to Milano, Florence, Rome, Vatican City, Pisa and Genoa, then Monaco and along the French Riviera to Nice, Cannes and Marseilles and on to Spain to see Barcelona, Velancia, Malaga, Gibraltar, Cadiz and Rota. We visited art museums, cathedrals, antique shops, ancient ruins and on and on and on. It was like a dream and Gene was the nicest person to be with in the whole world. How I loved him!

The trip refreshed us both and helped us look cheerfully ahead to his homecoming in just three short months. He came home in September and in a few weeks I realized that I was expecting again. On Halloween, we were serving trick or treaters at the door when I started hemorrhaging. My doctor was afraid I had miscarried but took the precaution of having me go to bed for two weeks with my feet elevated. I did exactly as he said, because I wanted to do everything I could to save my baby. During that time, Mark developed croup. I felt so helpless. His heavy breathing had awakened me in the night. I woke Gene and he brought Mark to me. While I comforted him, Gene ran hot water from the shower and carried Mark to the bathroom hoping the steam would relieve his breathing. I called our doctor and when he heard Mark's foghorn breathing from the bathroom, he said, "Get him to the hospital."

I could hear him as Gene carried him through the house and into the garage and I couldn't even be with him to comfort him but oh, how I prayed that night! He was gone five long days and were we ever happy to get back together!

While all of these things were going on Gene received orders to Norfolk, Virginia to be an aircraft accident investigator and we had to sell our home. When people came to look at it, the boys let them in, showed them through the house, and I sold it from my bed.

Early December brought a typical scene to Arlingwood Avenue. In every Navy town you grow accustomed to moving vans in front of houses with boxes, bicycles, mattresses and paraphernalia for living scattered all around. Wide-

30

eyed children watch as people scurry about being efficient. Gene was the efficient one in our household while I did my folding, packing and order giving from a chair. It was difficult watching everyone working so hard, but I had to be careful —my doctor still wasn't sure about our baby and had contacted a doctor in Norfolk for me to see soon after we arrived there.

Finally the last bed frame was taken out of the house; mops, brooms and a few lawn tools from the garage were packed into the remaining niche at the back of the moving van and the doors clanged shut. After securing the latch the driver climbed to his seat and off they went heading for Norfolk.

How hollow the house seemed.
Every footstep made a resounding echo.
Rooms that had been so cozy were barren now.
And we must leave our neighbors,
    Our friends,
    Our family of friends
We have shared our lives.

After the final cleaning of the house, we were all packed in the car and ready to leave but neighbors were there giving us cookies for the trip, reaching arms through the open windows to give us hugs or just standing there waving and wishing us well. The floodgates opened and I blubbered all the way to Georgia.

31

Chapter Five

Fit for Heaven

Every time we moved I started praying about our next home and neighborhood. Instead of praying specifically for a dream house that I built up in my mind, I asked God to do the selecting. We needed to live where He wanted us to live and the only way that could happen was to look at homes until He gave me a special heartwarming feeling of satisfaction when we walked through the right house. Gene waited patiently for my "This is it!" and then he smiled his approval.

While we were house hunting in Virginia Beach, the most wonderful sensation came over me and lifted my feelings sky high. As we were driving around, I put Gene's hand on my tummy and he felt it, too! Our baby was alive and kicking. My prayers had been answered and I was ever so thankful!

Being a member of the accident investigation team was a demanding job. Not only were they on call for major catastrophes, but minor aircraft problems had to be investigated also. Many times he would get in exhausted late at night only to be awakened by a phone call two or three hours into his deep sleep. I'd hear him come to attention and talk gravely about an accident in some far away state. Quickly he would shower, shave and get into a clean uniform while I put the coffee pot on and packed his duffel bag. He never left without going to the boys' beds and kissing them all goodbye and we never parted without a warm hug, kiss and "I love you!"

Our first and only daughter was born in Norfolk General hospital on June 2, 1962. I was jubilant! She even looked like a girl - all sweet and pretty and dainty with

eyelashes and a tiny nose. My heart was so full I could hardly contain myself. How could one woman be so blessed? When I thought of Gene and Bruce and Thomas and Mark and now our precious

Susan's first birthday

little Susan Elizabeth, I nearly burst as my tear ducts worked overtime again to release the pent-up love that filled my heart - it had to come out somewhere. Wasn't God good to plan for tears of joy and thanksgiving?

Mark and Susan

Three boys with a new baby sister
(Virginia Beach, Virginia)

33

Susan added her own special glow to our family. The boys loved her and helped care for her. Her cheerful disposition made it a pleasure to have her around and as soon as she could stand she started swaying and dancing to music. She loved her older brothers and was always caring for them - carrying shoes or whatever she thought they needed. Though she was very feminine she was very inquisitive about everything outside: bugs and toads, sticks and stones, butterflies and flowers. She loved to clean house with me and sit on the counter while I prepared food but then the boys loved to do that also - they all helped me bake bread, pies and cookies.

When Susan was six months old, my Dad had congestive heart failure and then a stroke. I went home and took Mark and Susan with me leaving Bruce and Thomas with Gene. After Dad was released from the hospital we all tried to go home as often as we could and then before we expected it, Gene had orders again.

Gene had an attractive "For Sale" sign made but never had time to hang it. We loved our home with its spacious rooms and an acre of lawn, but the time had come to get the sign out. So one Friday when I finished my weekly cleaning, I ran to the garage to get the sign and saying a prayer, placed it on the front porch propped against a large spinning wheel and I quickly arranged cut flowers in an antique crock and put it near the sign. Within minutes someone stopped and an hour later the house was sold - we took care of all the paperwork when Gene came home.

Our year in Fort Leavenworth was a wonderful interlude! Gene was one of three naval officers to be sent to the U.S. Army Command and General Staff College. We lived on the Post in cramped quarters and neighbors a few steps away, but we loved it! Our neighbors were wonderful and the fellow Navy officers became close friends. The boys were able to take advantage of the activities and facilities that were available. Two memorable things happened that year: President Kennedy was assassinated and we lived through a terrible tornado.

 34

We were all excited when Gene's orders took us back

to Virginia Beach because we knew our way around and we had friends there. Gene was going to be the Aircraft Assignment Officer on Air Lant Staff. We found a nice home in Kings Grant that seemed to have God's stamp of approval and we started to get settled in.

I am thankful that we had the life long habit of going to church on Sunday. Sometimes when we moved we would visit two or three churches before deciding on one, but this time we knew

My only brother

immediately, after our very first visit, that "This was the church for us!!

While we were getting adjusted to the changes that come with moving, we had a very upsetting call from home. My brother who was twenty-five had accidentally shot himself and was in the hospital. We were on our way!

Jim and I were very close - I had mothered him all his life. Our Mom had been sick the first few months after Jim was born so I had taken a lot of responsibility for a ten-year-old. I loved him and had a natural instinct to protect him. We could always talk to each other and I had been elated over the conversation we had had when Gene and I were home three weeks earlier. Jim had gone to see our Aunt Marguerite and after talking with her - he told me that he had accepted Christ. He had been anxious to tell me because he knew I was a Christian and he knew I wanted my family to know Christ also. Bless Aunt Marguerite's heart - she never minced words, as I do - she got right down to the meat of the issue and laid out the plan of salvation.

Jim died three days later; leaving not only a young wife and two boys, but also a family that dearly loved him.

35

Jim's death was a real turning point in my life. I wanted to make sure that my life would be fit for heaven so I could meet him there.

Mom and Dad were devastated by Jim's tragic death. I know it was harder for Mom because Jim had stopped in every day to spend time with both of them, but it especially helped her to have him cheer Dad up the way he did. Dad's stroke left him tearful and feeling useless. Dad was only fifty-seven.

Gene and I felt a deep concern for my parents so we made weekly trips to Pennsylvania. We would start the ten-hour trip as soon as Gene got home from work on Friday arriving home at 3:00 or 4:00 Saturday morning. I only slept two or three hours because I wanted to spend as much time with Mom and Dad as possible. We always had to leave Sunday morning to make the all day trip home.

Gene needed to be very alert at work because his duty was to keep track of every Navy plane in the Eastern Hemisphere and to position them. Every working person should have a day of rest but he never had time off during those weeks. He even had to do his required flight time at night because of his daytime workload.

After a few weeks of our strenuous schedule, we talked on our way back to Virginia about things that might encourage Mom and Dad. We began to think about our future in connection with them. Gene would have his twenty years in the Navy completed in May 1968 and then be able to retire. We talked about moving back to Pennsylvania and even though the question of where he would find work in that area concerned him, we agreed that my parents would be uplifted by such news. The only home and property that I could think of and felt good about was a place that I had known all my life. Mom's best friend, Hazel, and her husband were separated and had both left the area. Hazel lived in St. Petersburg, Florida. Hazel and Mom were lifelong friends - I think they met when they were in the eighth grade. Hazel even named me - my Grandfather Ayers (Dad's father) had told my parents that if they named me Sarah Adelaide after both my grandmothers, he would buy me the best baby carriage in the city of Elmira. Hazel visited Mom in the hospital the day I was born and said,

"Don't you dare do that to her - name her Jeanne Elizabeth!" So Mom did. (I'm happy with, or used to, my name but I also love my grandmother's names.) Hazel's place was only five miles over the hills from Mom and Dad's. We always called it a farm even though there hadn't been animals there for fifty or sixty years. There were 165 acres of rolling, hilly land that consisted of tillable fields (which a local farmer rented) and lots of woodland. There was even a large tree covered hill called Saxton's Knob. The comfortable home was nestled among trees on the corner of a county road and a dirt road. There wasn't another house in sight. The property had been in Hazel's family since 1785 and though Hazel had no dependents she vowed it would go up for Sheriff's auction before she would sell it. My brother, Jim, had even approached her about it soon after he married, but she said "No" and repeated her vow. The longer Gene and I talked about it, the more it seemed like the right thing to do but he said I would have to pray about it. We even set a price in our minds that we felt we could afford.

I had something new to talk to Jesus about and I was eager to begin. Making sure it was His will for us to consider this; praying about the financial burden that two house payments would surely impose on us; praying for Hazel to be ready to relinquish the responsibility; praying that it would encourage Mom and Dad and help heal the open wounds that they had.

A few months later when I called Hazel and told her our desire, she said, "I would have never sold it to anyone else." And then when she told me the price I nearly squealed! It was the exact price Gene and I had talked about.

Mom and Dad were elated when we told them our plans and they began healing. I was thankful for the new experiences we were having in our church because I could openly share with my parents the fresh insight I was gleaning from my Bible Study and to talk about my desire to serve and be used by God. Dad started praying for others and found that the days that Mom was teaching school were no longer lonely. He would call me and tell me about his peace and joy. He gave his heart to Jesus and I gave Jesus my heartfelt thanksgiving for answering my prayers and working every detail out so beautifully.

37

Chapter Six

Her Real Birthday

We were thankful for our comfortable Virginia Beach home: the peaceful neighborhood, the wonderful friends (some of whom were from our Jacksonville days) and we loved our new church. Not only did we attend church almost immediately, we were also involved. The minister and his wife became our friends and Gene's and my Sunday School teacher, Burnett, was exactly what we needed for he was a brilliant student of the Bible who was caring, warm and compassionate. He and his wife, Ramona, were graduates of Houghton College and they were tremendously helpful to both of us. She was my Bible Study teacher and a dear friend. Those Tuesday mornings in her home were especially nourishing because they came at a time of rededication in my life when I had a hearty appetite for everything she was teaching. The women in that Bible Study became my sisters in Christ. The children loved their Sunday School teachers, the fellowship dinners and their friends. Gene joined the Men's Club and I was the choir director. The choir members crept right into my heart.

One of my best friends was Dolly Fischer. Her husband, Bob, was a tall, rugged Marine with a mellow baritone voice and he loved to sing, so the very first week they visited our church, he joined the choir. Dolly and I were immediate friends and soon discovered that we were very much alike. We would get tearful when we talked about our husbands and children and seemed to have similar devotion to them. We loved to keep house, bake and plan special meals for our families. We endured Military protocol, parties and social events. Neither of us drank or smoked so we could have felt uncomfortable but each of us had husbands that admired and respected us for what we were - so we felt strengthened by them.

38

Friends forever – Jeanne, Edie and Dolly

Dolly started going to our Bible Study and was such a delightful addition to our group. (My girlfriend, Edie and I took her right under our wing and we became an inseparable threesome!) In all of Dolly's travels she had never had the opportunity to belong to a Bible Study so she became an eager participant.

Dolly was one of those special people whose heart was in tune with the needs of people. She was always sending cards or taking cookies to a shut-in, helping a neighbor or (in her gentle, quiet way) being an encouragement to someone. Her concern for others was always overflowing. She didn't gossip, was always trustworthy and never had a biting tongue. She was truly a good person.

One Sunday we had a guest speaker at church and he said, "If I asked how many of you are Christians, I'm sure most of you would raise your hands. If I asked how do you know you are a Christian there would be many answers such as: I go to church; I read my Bible; my grandfather was a minister; I teach Sunday School; I'm not a Jew so I'm a Christian; I try to be a good person and on and on. But how many of you would say - Because I have a personal relationship with Jesus?" Then he explained about receiving Christ.

39

The next Tuesday morning we started the book of John in our Bible Study and spent a good deal of time on verse 12: "But to all who received Him, who believed in His name, He gave power to become children of God."

All of these things began to stir Dolly and she shared with me that after all those years of thinking she was a Christian she began to wonder if she really was because she had never asked Jesus to fill her heart. I simply said, "If you're not sure - make sure!" Two days later it was her birthday and before I could call her to wish her a happy day, she called me. She was crying, but I could feel her joy shining through her tears. She said, "This is my real birthday - I just asked Jesus to come into my heart!"

How can such a good person be transformed? I saw it with my own eyes. She became radiant and all her good qualities were magnified and made excellent because they were refined by the fruits of the Holy Spirit. She was suddenly attached to Jesus - like a branch to the vine and she knew it! (John 15:1-8)

My dear, sweet friend, Dolly, my sister in Christ, died of cancer a number of years ago. But even during her suffering her thoughts were on others and she had no fear of death because she knew she was going to heaven to be with Jesus. She also knew her family would someday be there with her because she had been faithful and she had led them to Christ.

41

Chapter Seven

Self Pity

The very best years that I had during Gene's Navy career were the years that he was on shore duty so that tour on Air Lant Staff was one of those special times. I very easily fell into the wonderful routine of having him come home every night and the children loved it, too. We always greeted him the same way. I had dinner cooking and the table set, the house was straightened and so was I. Mark and Susan watched for him and made the announcement so we could all be there to greet him when he came in the door. After a pleasant dinner we had devotions at the kitchen table and then we did dishes. We loved our evenings with the children and they especially looked forward to the weekends with Daddy home.

But that ended all too soon. Gene was accepted as a prospective Commanding Officer and with that came orders to train in the F4 Phantom II. What a privilege! At that time the F4 was the most capable fighter interceptor in the free world. Its top speed was Mach 2.4 or about 1600 miles per hour. He went to Key West to train for two months and then back to Oceana, VA which was the home base of VF102, the squadron he would be in for the next two years; one as Executive Officer and the second year as Commanding Officer.

Sometimes before Gene left on a long nine month cruise I would get withdrawn and quiet because of my anxiety over what seemed overwhelming responsibility with no relief in caring for the children, the home - everything! Thoughts of how much I would miss him made me tearful. It always seemed to me that he was so strong that he wasn't dreading it as I was - besides he loved flying. How many times when we stood in

Accepting Command of VF-102

the moonlight together had he said, "It's a great night for night-flying?" So I built up a little resentment and because I knew I would cry if I talked about it I would just hold it inside. I remember one night after we went to bed he said we had better pray about it.

When I heard his heartfelt prayer of concern for us, his recognition of my responsibilities, his admiration for the way I carried out my duties and his reluctance in hav-

ing to be away from his family - all of my self pity left. When he heard me ask the Lord for forgiveness for all my weaknesses he understood me better and did all he could to protect me from the things that troubled me. The heartfelt prayers of a man and wife are so pleasing to the Lord and nothing is more healing.

The fall months of 1966 were busy ones. Gene was in Key West. I was starting work on the Christmas cantata at church and I also headed up a Craft Bazaar to earn money for choir robes. Every spare minute I would get some cookies or finger food baked and frozen as I planned ahead for the choir caroling party that we had every year in our home. It was a beautiful Christmas season because Gene finished his training and came home to enjoy the holidays with us. Christmas is such a joyous time when it is truly the celebration of the birth of Christ.

On January 3rd 1967 we had to take Gene to the airport to fly to the Mediterranean where he joined his squadron aboard the USS America. You would think that I would have grown used to separations but they just got harder each time. My heart was heavy and yet I tried to be strong for Gene and the children when we said goodbye, but when I went to bed that night I just fell apart. Even after I went to sleep it would seem like he was there but then my heart would ache again when I realized it was only his pillow that still smelled like him.

Writing to Gene had always been a source of comfort to me. Not only was it a good time to keep him abreast of the family news and all our varied activities but also it was my quiet time with him when I could express my feelings and be closer drawn to him. This time it wasn't easy to even start the letters. I'd write the date at the top and then sit there trying to get started but I couldn't - I had nothing to write. Each night I used the same paper - scratched off the date and wrote the next one.

After a week I started putting thoughts on paper but nothing sounded right - my "hope you're having fun" sounded sarcastic and when I wrote "I'd rather you be a garbage collector and be home every night!" I knew I couldn't mail that so my letters ended up in the wastebasket - all tear stained with tears of self-pity.

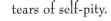

44

Even when you know Jesus and want to serve him with your whole heart, it is difficult to overcome all the filth of your sinful nature. The big dark cloud that was hovering over my heart was plugging up the filters. The Sonlight wasn't getting in and for sure - it couldn't shine out. I was praying for others each day; having devotions with the children; doing all the church work I was involved in; directing the choirs (I had three by this time); filling my Navy Wives Club obligations; caring for the house and children and performing as I and others expected me to but the treadmill was wearing me out - I felt exhausted!

Why do we make life so difficult for ourselves? Why do we avoid admitting that we have a problem? Why do we not make use of all the promises we have as Christians? Jesus sent us a Comforter to abide with us, strengthen us, equip us to serve, give us hope and to make us Christ-like!

As I turned to Him in prayer - two weeks after Gene left - I was begging His forgiveness. I was so sorry. I had been submitting only the things I was proud of to Him and trying to hide my weaknesses from everyone - even Him. I wanted a clean heart and only He could cleanse it. I cried tears of shame and then they turned into tears of joy as I felt His forgiveness and tender mercy fill my heart.

My writing pad was in my lap and when I picked it up to start my letter to Gene the Lord gave me a song instead. It is called The Green Valley.

> There is a green valley just over the hill
> Where peace, joy and laughter come into your heart.
> If you want to go there - you can and you will
> Just say, "Lord, I'm Yours," and your new life will start.

Refrain:
> Come to the green valley - it's open to all
> Come in and be filled with His wonderful love
> Come all ye who yearn to bow down at His feet
> He'll bless you and keep you for glory above.

> When you reach that hilltop and look down below
> You'll see the green valley and then you will know
> That Jesus the Savior has set it aglow
> His grace and His beauty will enter your soul.

45

Refrain: *Come to the green valley - it's open to all*
Come in and be filled with His wonderful love
Come all ye who yearn to bow down at His feet
He'll bless you and keep you for glory above.

Now walk down that hillside right into His light
Look up in His face and He'll cleanse you within
Then sing of His praises from morning till night
For life will be sweet as you walk on with Him!

Refrain: *Come to the green valley - it's open to all*
Come in and be filled with His wonderful love
Come all ye who yearn to bow down at His feet
He'll bless you and keep you for glory above.

After I wrote the song and melody down I was able to write joy filled letters of encouragement to Gene for the remainder of the nine months. I can still remember how crystal clear the blessings were from then on. When I went in that night to kiss all of the children, check their covers and rearrange toys in Mark and Susan's beds so they could have more freedom to move and as I prayed for each one of them, my cup was running over. What a privilege that the Lord had entrusted me with their care. What a priceless gift they were to me! I prayed that each would know and love the Lord and my prayers of gratitude for what they meant to me - brought me to tears again.

The next morning everything seemed so much easier. With my burden lifted I even had more energy. Breakfast was fun, clean up was speedy and after the three boys went to school; Susan and I cleaned house. We even got some of the inside windows washed that morning. Then in the afternoon, when it warmed up, while Susan played on the swing set, I washed the outside windows to let the sunshine in.

We grow closer to God when we confess our sins, ask His forgiveness and let him blow away the dark cloud that smothers us. We must clear the way for God to do greater works in our lives.

46

In my mind Jesus worked a miracle in me that night. When He heard my cry and took away my weakness of self-pity He really erased it from my life!

The next year Gene was shot down over Vietnam and I am so thankful I didn't have to waste my time and life on the added burden of self-pity! I was set free because my faith had been made stronger and I knew that even though our family was to suffer this unknown - the six of us would be held tightly together because "His grace is sufficient and His power is perfected in weakness." II Corinthians 12:9 & 10

Chapter Eight

Time

In late May I received a telegram from Gene asking me to meet him on 1 July in Athens, Greece for 22 days. Again I wondered how I could leave the children but Gene was serious! So off I drove to Pennsylvania to leave the children with Mom and Dad and then I flew to Athens. It was another beautiful reunion and a wonderful adventure.

We walked for miles through antiquity that seemed to thrust us into another world. Here in the United States we live in such a new nation that to us Civil War era is old; but there Gene and I stood in the Parthenon, the Doric temple of Athena, built on the Acropolis in the fifth century before Christ. We took in as many of the sights as possible in the few days that the ship was in port, but then it was time for Gene to go back aboard. The ship would work its way up to Thessalonica where it would anchor in ten days.

Fortunately there were five or six other squadron wives staying in the same hotel so I had a good opportunity to get acquainted with them and make friends. It would have been difficult to be alone in Greece because of the language. In other European countries where we traveled it seemed you could pick out a word here and there that was similar to English and perhaps the little bit of Latin and French that I learned in high school had helped me, but Greek was "all Greek" to me!

I have always been in the habit of getting up early (around 5:30) and the other girls liked to sleep in. I studied the city bus route with the desk clerk one morning and decided (with his notes of instruction) to make my way across the city to a United States installation that had a Post Exchange. As I made the long journey, different people got on and off

the bus but at one stop a pleasant woman got on and sat beside me. We exchanged smiles and words of greeting that neither of us understood so we laughed and rode in silence. As I looked out the window I saw an impressive, stately church ahead. As we passed it I pointed it out to her, then gestured to my heart and said, "I am a Christian." She burst into nods of understanding saying something that sounded like "Jesu Christi" to me. Then she pulled at a chain around her neck and out came a cross. I touched it and we were both smiling, laughing and nodding. We hugged each other when she left the bus knowing we were forever united by Christ.

Another wife and I drove to Thessalonica where Gene and I had a few more days together. Wherever we walked we wondered if the Apostle Paul had walked that same path. We found wonderful restaurants and shopped for antique buttons and copper in crowded little shops. We bought a few pieces of copper and then saw a large tub that Mom would enjoy keeping her magazines in near her wing chair by the fireplace. The smaller items fit neatly inside the tub so we each took a handle in hand and proceeded to wind our way around the people on the sidewalks. When we saw an even larger copper tub for ourselves, we tested to see if the large one would fit inside the larger tub. It did so we bought it. By then we had such a heavy and awkward load that we felt it was necessary to go out to the ship and store it in Gene's stateroom.

I didn't realize what a hair-raising experience it would be to get on the ship. Over the years I had been on and off aircraft carriers countless times. Every other time the ship was moored to the pier where nothing was moving. The gangway from the pier to the main deck was wide with easy stride steps and handrails on each side - everything was safe and secure. There was a certain elegance and a stirring of patriotism as you walked up and neared the wide entrance of the main deck with the flight deck overhanging above, flags flying and uniformed men standing at attention, saluting your arrival. When you stepped on the ship the enormity was breathtaking and then you entered the carpeted quarterdeck where plaques and pictures were displayed. But this day in Greece was different - very different.

49

The officers' launch, which held ten or twelve passengers, came from the ship to pick us up at the landing. The ship was quite a distance out in the bay and generally the water was very choppy but the further we got from shore the harder it was to make headway because we were in white capped swells. The closer we got to the aircraft carrier the larger it looked and the higher the waves became but we made it and hovered near its side. The launch was tied up against the ship that loomed overhead and looked a mile high. Two enlisted men were on a platform at the foot of the gangway ladder that went about forty feet up the side of the ship to the main deck. The ship was steady but the launch was bobbing not only up and down but also towards and away from the side of the ship. When the launch was away from the ship the gap was fearsome. I put my life in Gene's hands and had to trust that this husband of mine knew exactly when the right time to jump came. He watched the bobbing and when the "up" synchronized with the "towards" he threw me into the attentive arms of the seamen. Then he passed our copper cargo to the men before he easily made the jump himself. By the time we climbed the narrow gangway ladder, each holding a handle of the copper tub, up the side of the ship and onto the main deck I didn't know if I should breathe a sigh of relief or faint. I decided to breathe the sigh because I didn't want Gene to think I was a wimp.

I tried to enjoy our time aboard by not thinking ahead to our departure from the ship. Then we would have to go down the ladder seeing the turbulence below and the gaping hole into the depths of the sea that appeared each time the bouncing launch made its rhythmic move away from the ship. Then there would be the dreaded leap from the platform to the seesawing launch praying every minute that your feet would reach the solid bottom of the boat instead of being swallowed up by the biting waves beneath.

They say it is good for you to do things that will quicken your heartbeat. Given a choice I would run in place on a firm and resilient floor rather than go down the side of a ship. I guess I have been a little facetious in the telling of this story because I must admit that even though it caused my heart to pound —I treasure the memory. It was a wonderful adventure and I never once was worried because Gene was there to

take care of me. I knew that he would do anything to protect me and keep me from harm.

Thank You, Lord, for my treasure of a husband. Thank You for his strong arms that hold me; and thank You even more that Your loving arms encircle us both. We love You, Jesus!

We both returned to Athens - one by sea and one by land and after another short stay in Athens, we flew to Brindisi, Italy on an Airforce plane. Then on to Rome where we both caught planes that would take us in different directions: Gene flew east to Athens and I flew west, back to the happy arms of our children. Gene returned to the U.S. just a few weeks later.

The children and I were excited about getting back to our home in Virginia Beach. We were all anxious to settle in and get together with friends again but as a family, we couldn't wait for our mornings at the beach. We had been doing it since each of them was very young and it was our special time together. We would all get up early, have breakfast, do dishes, make our beds, and get dressed in swimsuits and T-shirts. I would pack snacks, fruits and beverages in a small cooler while they got their sand buckets and shovels in the trunk. All we had to do was grab the stack of clean beach towels and we were on our way - singing all the way to the beach. We had our favorite place and since we were generally the first ones to arrive we were able to stake out our claim and mark our area by spreading our beach towels and digging the shovels into the sand where we would be building castles. But first things first - early morning is the best time to look for unusual shells, so, with buckets in hand, we would walk far down the beach, near the water's edge where the sand was firm and the gentle morning tide moved in and out on our feet. We loved the peace, the gentle sound of the lapping ocean, the damp, slightly fishy smell of salt water, and the sun on our shoulders. At intervals we would stop to talk to the man who was casting for fish. Or we stood shielding our eyes against the sun in the eastern sky as we watched a school of porpoise gently rolling through the ocean showing off their glistening, rounded backs as they followed one after the other with the exception of the occasional playful scholar that frolicked and cavorted by leaping high in the air. Or

51

we spoke to the older lady that always took her brisk morning walk - her skin was like brown tanned leather and she wore a big floppy straw hat. We loved each other, too. We didn't talk about it but sometimes we held hands as we walked. When we turned back to retrace our melting footprints, we could see our towels. We walked faster because it was time to start the castle and get on with our morning work that consisted of swimming, playing in the water, running in the sand, eating a snack and lying in the sun.

While the children worked on the castle, I frequently retreated to my towel to sit there and watch them - what blessings they were! How the big boys were growing! Gene would love to be with us! I was so grateful for him! And thankful I could have these special mornings at the beach with our children! Life was good!

I had time to think that summer and pray about the changes that were coming into our lives. With Gene's position as Executive Officer came added social responsibility and we were expected to be involved in everything. During this period of time, before Gene returned, a Navy wife, who didn't know us very well, talked to me about my personal stand against drinking. She warned me that it could interfere with Gene's promotion to Commanding Officer. Do you wonder that I needed to pray? I was deeply concerned because I would never do anything to hinder Gene's progress and always tried to be an encouragement to him. Why should our not drinking or not serving it in our home cause a problem? I loved the people Gene worked with; we truly were not judgmental of those who drank and we always felt that they accepted us and didn't feel the slightest bit uncomfortable around us.

Praying only strengthened my decision to not serve alcohol in our home. How could we change? To me, I would be hurting God if I started to do something that He had given me such a strong conviction not to do. My aim - my purpose in life is to please Him and never ever do anything to hurt Him. Surely He would sustain us through the changes that were to come!

This whole thought process took me back in time. When Gene and I were first married and were traveling to

California, Gene tried to prepare me for Navy life by telling me about social calls, cocktail parties and happy hours after work on Friday. None of those things surprised me. I had gone to college and had friends who drank and besides that, I grew up around drinking. When I accepted Christ, He gave me a strong conviction. I knew I never wanted alcohol in my home! This was a personal decision that I kept to myself, it didn't mean that I didn't like people who drank - on the contrary, I loved the people in my family who did but I couldn't see any good that came from it. In fact, I saw a lot of bad that came from it. Also when I gave my life to Jesus, I wanted to live in such a way that my life would reflect Him (not that I could ever be worthy) but He loved me and I wanted my life to show how much I loved Him. I didn't want any of my actions to cause people to question the sincerity of my walk with Christ. Gene had known that I wanted our home to be free of alcohol but I reaffirmed it on our trip. He was thinking about some of his bachelor friends and asked if they could bring their own bottle when we invited them for dinner and I gave my reasons for not telling them they could. Though Gene didn't have my strong convictions, he loved me enough to not only agree but to stand firm with me. Those bachelors came for dinner the second or third Saturday night after we moved into that first apartment. We had a wonderful evening; they thoroughly enjoyed the home cooked food and lively conversation. Gene even prayed before dinner - a tradition we started with our first meal together and we held hands around the table! They came often and after we were settled in Kingsville, two of them came there with their new wives. We all became good friends.

I was thankful that the summer of '67 had provided me with time; time with Gene, time with the children and time to pray, reflect and build for the future.

53

Chapter Nine

Precious Minutes

That September our church started a Kindergarten class and I was pleased to know that Susan would be with a dedicated Christian teacher that she already knew and loved. All of her very best friends were in her class, so school was like going to a birthday party everyday. She just loved it and though I missed having her with me, I loved seeing her so happy. Now she was a big girl and went to school just like her brothers. The boys loved their schools also and each of them had wonderful friends. They were involved in church, youth group, scouts, band and piano lessons.

Gene's added responsibilities kept him running. As he was finishing his year as Executive Officer his orders came in to take over Command of the squadron and we learned that within days of the change of command ceremony (29 March 1968), they were to deploy to Vietnam aboard the USS America (10 April 1968). Preparations for combat tightened his schedule. They were flying every day and many nights. They were doing air combat maneuvers, a contemporary term for dog fighting, maneuvering against missiles or aircraft. In mid-winter the carrier had to deploy to Puerto Rico; that meant the air wing (the group of squadrons attached to the ship) had to go also.

While the ship was in Puerto Rico, I went to the Officers Club to make arrangements for Gene's change of command reception. I prayed hard before I went. Gene and I had talked it over and decided on a morning ceremony to help alleviate the expectancy of alcoholic beverages at the reception. The woman that helped me at the O Club was pleased when I ordered more than the average finger foods and hors d'oeuvres but when it came time to talk about beverages, she was ap-

palled when I ordered fruit punch. Champagne and Bloody Mary's were in order. When she became insistent because official dignitaries would be there, I very politely stood and said, "That's all right, I can have it in our home." She realized then that I was serious. I was pleasant but firm. As we finished the plans she became friendlier and she told me that there had never been a change of command reception at the O Club without alcohol. (We were friends by the time the reception was over and she was very pleased to see how much our guests enjoyed themselves.)

With the arrangements for the reception completed I had to start planning and preparing for the open house which would be in our home for Gene's officers and their wives. I love giving a party from the planning, inviting the guests, preparing the food, cleaning the house, setting the tables, arranging the flowers - right down to lighting the candles throughout the house before the guests arrive. The dining room table

On our way to the Change of Command Ceremony.

was filled with punch bowl, chafing dishes and trays filled with finger foods, shrimp, ham and sweet and sour meatballs. The homemade pastries, bundt cakes and cheesecakes were on the kitchen table with coffee and tea on the counter.

Someone sat down and started playing the piano while others gathered around to sing. There were people in the dining room, music room, kitchen, living room and some even sat on the floor near the fireplace in the family room. As people left, we hugged. They enjoyed it and so did we! Gene and I had already grown to love those men and their wives.

The ship had been in Puerto Rico from January 16 to February 11 and then they were out on the ship again for maneuvers from March 7 to March 22. Gene's workload was increasing every day and I was desperate for us to have family time so that he could be with the children. Yet the calendar was mushrooming and the blocks for each day filled and spilled over to the next so I had to write notes all around the margin. Not only did we have the Change of Command Reception and Open House to think about; but on March 23, the outgoing CO and his wife had their party, and a few days later, the Air Wing had its huge dinner party at the O Club. Something was going on nearly every night but at least the children, Gene and I were having breakfast, dinner, devotions, church and Sundays together. I secured as many time frames as I could for us to be alone as a family and the last night before he left

56   *Change of Command Ceremony*

was off limits for everyone! I couldn't believe it when at dinnertime the phone rang and Gene went in the family room to talk - I could hear him saying, "But this is my last night with my family." Gene really tried but he could not be rude to an old acquaintance. The man was coming right over; he wanted to see Gene before he left for Vietnam. Normally I am very sociable, but that night was a real struggle for me. Gene took him to the living room while the children and I did dishes then sat together in the family room. They took their baths, then we waited in the family room again and then it was past time for Mark and Susan to go to bed. They kissed Daddy goodnight and went to bed.

When the man finally left at 10:30 Bruce and Thomas were still standing in the bedroom hallway listening for his departure so they could have a tired moment with their Dad. Tears welled in my eyes when I watched them. I was hurt but I couldn't be angry and ruin our last precious minutes with each other.

Chapter Ten

Goodbye is Very Hard to Say

All too soon morning came and it was an extra early morning that memorable day of April 10, 1968. After we loaded Gene's last minute gear in the trunk (most of his things were already on the carrier) he drove us out to the airfield at NAS Oceana. We made our way to the VF102 hangar where the jets were lined up ready to go. The USS America was home ported at NAS Norfolk and usually the planes were already aboard at the time of departure but VF 102 had received some new planes right up until the last day, so they had to fly aboard after the carrier was underway. Once that was accomplished, the ship would start its long journey to Vietnam via South America, around the Cape of South Africa, through the Indian Ocean to the Philippines.

Gene took us to a lounge next to the ready room. The large room where the dependents would gather had sofas and chairs in groupings throughout the room. Gene had to leave us there because much had to be done in preparation for take off and also in leaving their hangar space for nine months.

The couples and families started arriving. There were hushed greetings as each family came in. I couldn't help but notice that a change had come over the men - the jovial, boisterous, camaraderie was gone because a gentle, compassionate warmth had taken over. Each family found their own little corner or section of the room where they could be together until departure time. One couple just gazed out the window holding hands; children hugged their Daddy while the tearful wife looked on. One man squatted on his haunches in front of his wife while she sat in a chair and as he held her hands and looked deep into her eyes, they talked intently. Toddlers hugged Daddy's leg while he gave last

minute instructions to his wife. Each little group gave off its own message that goodbye is very hard to say.

As I looked from family to family I said a little prayer for each of them and then my eyes rested on Bernie, Reidun and their ten-month-old daughter, Michelle. When Gene was Executive Officer, Bernie had been his RIO (radar intercept officer). The F4 is a tandem seated jet with the pilot in front and the RIO in the back seat. Bernie was a Lt.jg and when Gene became CO he had the option of having the most senior RIO, but Gene opted to keep Bernie because he was good and they worked well together. Bernie had married a Norwegian citizen who had come to the U.S. to work in his hometown. Reidun and I became good friends while they were in the Mediterranean and she was expecting, so we loved their daughter Michelle right from the start. Bernie and Reidun had a little Mustang that found its way into our driveway quite often and our children would run to greet them.

As I looked around the room, I felt compassion for each couple and family. My heart would knot up when I saw Em (who was Gene's wing man), Carolyn and their daughter Amy, but that was just because I loved them. When I looked at Bernie, Reidun and Michelle, I'd have to quickly look away because tears would come to my eyes and I didn't want Gene to find me crying - he had enough on his mind. The children and I kept waiting for him. When he finally came, it was to say goodbye. We all clung to each other for as long as we could and then it was over.

We left the hangar, one part of us missing, and walked to the car. Methodically I drove off the base and started the drive down the long, fairly isolated stretch of highway that led back to Virginia Beach. We could hear the roar of the jets as they revved up their engines and I couldn't endure it any longer. I had to pull the car off the road and with my head on my arms over the steering wheel; I broke into a sobbing cry. The roaring jets took off and sliced through the sky. I always tried to be strong for the children but they understood because they felt the same way. We all had a huddle hug before we regained our composure and drove home.

In my mind I had a specific mission as the "Skippers" wife. Gene left with 42 officers and 240 enlisted men in his squadron. The Lord gave me a heavy burden, and a great love for each of their wives. I truly wanted to serve them, help them and be an encouragement to them. Soon after the ship was underway I planned a potluck picnic for the enlisted wives at a park on the grounds at NAS Oceana. We met and after the meal I talked to them as they gathered close by - some on benches and some sitting on the grass. Some were newlyweds, but most had been Navy wives for a few years and had children.

I talked to them about the fine men they were married to and about the added stress the men would be under. I talked about loving, encouraging and protecting their husbands and urged them to write every day. Then I talked about loyalty and keeping themselves for the untarnished return of their husband. I even told them that going to the Enlisted Club on weekends was the last thing they should do - by drowning their sorrows they would be weakening their values and subjecting themselves to improper behavior that could only cause regrets. They needed to be involved in their children's lives as well as each other. They could under-gird and be a lifeline to one another by planning regular get-togethers that included their children, starting bowling leagues, or just having gab sessions over coffee. Chapel or church on Sunday would strengthen them and help them get through each week. I shared with them about my love for Gene, how we prayed for each other and were kept together by God.

After I met with the enlisted wives, I did the same thing at a potluck dinner for the officer's wives. I also talked to them about the serious subject of what steps had to be taken if there should be an accident. The law of averages let us know that because of combat, at least two and possibly three of the planes would be shot down. The enlisted men were relatively safe aboard the carrier but the officers would all be flying in combat and were open targets. We had definite cause to be there for each other! As I talked to them I never dreamed that Gene would be the first to be shot down.

60

Preparing flight plan aboard USS America (June 1968)

Proverbs 3: 5-6

Trust in the Lord with all your heart and lean not on your own understanding, in all your ways acknowledge Him and He shall direct your paths.

Think about these words - this isn't part time commitment - this is *full-time trust* (knowing Him personally, being in fellowship with Him and leaning on Him instead of our own understanding.) To acknowledge God is to be ever mindful of Him and to serve Him with a willing and faithful heart. Then - He will direct our paths by making them straight, clearing them of obstacles, lifting us over the rough places and enabling us to go forward.

Isn't He wonderful?

These verses are appropriate before I begin our POW story because you need to realize that I firmly believed in Jesus and trusted Him with all my heart when Gene left for Vietnam. I am so thankful for His great love - if we hadn't been a Christian family our story would not have been the same. As I relate it to you, I *pray* that *God* will be glorified.

61

Great Is Thy Faithfulness

PART TWO

"GREAT IS THY FAITHFULNESS"

Chapter Eleven

Missing In Action

When Gene left in April 1968, Gene and I were 38, Bruce was 14, Thomas was 12, Mark was 7 and Susan was 5. As you know, my days were full and the responsibilities great but I was able to keep the pace and do it calmly and with joy because the Lord gave me the energy and the desire.

On June 5th, my life started to change. At 5:00 PM I was getting ready for an Air Wing Wives dinner party. I was hostess and had to get to the Officer's Club early to decorate the tables. The children's meal was on the stove and the table was set for them. The phone rang and I could hardly understand my mother - she was hysterical. She had bus duty and had been detained at school and then came home to find my Dad dead on the dining room floor. I tried to calm her and told her we would be right home. I asked if she had called the doctor - she hadn't so I told her what to do but she dropped the phone - I had no idea what happened to her and my attempts to get her back on the line were futile. I called my Aunt Ruth in Elmira, told her about Dad and asked if she and Uncle Bob would go to Mom immediately. She said they would.

Now if Jeanne Wilber had been in control, I would have gone and thrown myself on my bed to mourn for my treasure of a Dad. But Jesus was there! He took over! I notified the Executive Officer's wife about taking over the responsibilities at the dinner party, called my minister and gave him a plan for special music for the next few Sundays, called my Bible Study teacher and dictated a telegram to her to send to Gene. The children and I cleaned the kitchen and refrigerator and took perishable food to our neighbor asking her to notify the paper and post office; and asked her to water the plants. Then the children helped fold the clothes in the dryer and we packed clothes for six weeks.

At 6:30 we were on our way. No one can tell me that we could have done all that in one and one-half hours without the Lord's help and we were all aware of His loving presence in our car during the ten-hour trip home. (Bobby Kennedy was shot that night so we listened to that on the radio and prayed for his family.) We arrived home at 4:30 AM and only He could have helped me comfort Mom and keep me alert enough to make the funeral arrangements and stay awake until nearly midnight the next night.

Eleven days later it was Father's Day, June 16, 1968. The children, Mom and I went to church in the morning, had a quiet dinner before friends and relatives came to call in the afternoon. It wasn't an easy day, but we got through the day with peace and a great deal of love.

After the children went to bed that night, Mom and I stayed up late and for some reason, I couldn't stop talking about Gene. At exactly midnight the doorbell rang. I went to the door and let in two uniformed men who had asked if I was Mrs. Wilber. As I held the door for them to enter the kitchen, my heart was already pounding. I knew their mission. As we stood in the kitchen where Gene had first told me he loved me, I got the tragic news that he was Missing In Action - his plane had not returned to the ship. (This is not news you want to hear!) I tried to get more information from them but they said it was classified and they did not know anymore. (One of the letters I received from Gene three or four days prior to this told me about a plane that had gone into the water during takeoff from the carrier. The two men did not have time to eject so they went under with the plane. Because the bodies were not retrieved, the men were

listed as Missing In Action - so you see I needed to know the circumstances.) I said, "Gene had to have been shot down - my husband is too good a pilot to have crashed!" They just looked at me. I remember how my heart ached for them - having to come out in the middle of the night to be bearers of such bad news.

I kept grasping for something to cling to. Finally I said, "Well, there's hope?!" No answer. I sat down at the kitchen table and put my head down on my folded arms. Lt. Lewis looked at Mom and shook his head and I lifted mine in time to see it. He asked me if they should stop at Gene's parents to notify them, but I was concerned at how it would affect them if they were awakened and had no one around to help them, so I asked that they be notified at 8:00 in the morning. (Gene's sister and her husband lived next door to them.) They also asked if I needed a doctor because I had turned icy cold but I assured them I would be fine. They left.

I decided not to awaken the children. I would wait until 7:00 AM and by then, I would have the strength to comfort them. I would need to pray for them. They already had a great burden trying to deal with the loss of their Grampy who had always put a special spark in their lives. And now they had to be told about their beloved Dad. (Oh, precious Lord, help me!)

Mom tried to get me to go to bed but I couldn't rest or even sit still. I have never been so cold and I shook uncontrollably. Mom put blankets around my shoulders but I couldn't get warm. I just walked the floor and kept saying, "Gene is my life!"

Toward morning I stood looking out of the picture window in the den. It was still dark. For the first time in my life I couldn't utter a prayer. Jesus knew I loved Him - I always felt when I talked to Him about everything in my life that I needed to reaffirm my love for Him but now I was silent and yet I still felt His wonderful love. In my silence - my inability to pray intelligently, the Holy Spirit interceded for me (Romans 8:26). I looked out at the dark sky and in my mind's eye I lifted my broken heart to him. I needed to know if Gene was alive. Suddenly I felt a warmth all through me. He lifted my burden. He took away the pain. He mended my broken heart. I walked in the living room and told Mom, "Gene is alive!"

Now I truly understood the 'Peace that passes all understanding.' The Lord helped me tell the children in the morning. I am so grateful He had given me that hope that I longed for before I talked to them. The Lord was my strength as I told them and their strength as they heard it. How fortunate I was to have such gentle trusting children. We were encompassed by His love.

An hour later my girlfriend called from Virginia Beach to read me an article in the morning newspaper - air search and rescue from the USS America was trying to locate the two men who were in a Phantom F4J that was shot down north of the DMZ. The men were not identified but Edie new it was a plane from Gene's squadron. She was grief stricken when I told her it was Gene's plane, but I was glad she called. This confirmed what the Lord had let me know during the night and now I knew something about the circumstances. She said she would start the prayer chain in Virginia Beach.

That day I found the 91st Psalm which was my comfort - it assured me that Gene would be protected. On that day also I felt very strongly that Jesus needed to use Gene there. That night when Susan said her prayers it touched me that the Lord led her to feel the same way. She said, "Dear Jesus, help Daddy to be safe. Help the good men to find him, but if the bad men find him - help Daddy to make them good. Bring him back to us. I love you Jesus, Amen."

People were wonderful. Our family and friends around us in Pennsylvania came to console and help; our minister who was a family friend and officiated at Jim and Dad's funerals was there every day to support us. Friends from Virginia Beach called every day and some made the long trip up to be with us. Thomas' birthday was three days after Gene was shot down and my heart ached for him - such a fine boy. He was thirteen and I wanted it to be a perfect time for him. He could have been

pouty and disagreeable, but he wasn't. He was loving and apprecia-tive of the small endeavor that I made. How can one woman be so blessed?

One of the couples who came up from Virginia Beach was very helpful. While she stayed with me, her husband (who was a good friend of Gene's) took the children to the creek to go swim-ming in the swimming hole that I had spent much time in when I was a young teenager. Thomas dove in and lost his glasses. After a trip up the hill to tell me about it they all returned to the creek and our friend was able to find the glasses - whew! It was good to have some normal realistic excitement.

It didn't take much to make us cry. One family member's tears would set off an avalanche that quickly spread to the rest of us which gave each of us cause to comfort the other and try to get us back in control again. The children and I prayed fervently for Gene and we were always thankful for God's protection and strength for Gene and for us. The loving bond that we always had was even stronger now.

During my personal prayers for Gene I realized that I had never relinquished him to the Lord. I guess I always wanted to pull a few of the strings and it took my complete inability to do that - to make me realize that it was something I had to do. I loved him more. Though I didn't have proof that Gene would be a POW, I started praying that they would not torture him. The more I read Psalm 91, the more I thought about angels and Ramona, my Bible Study teacher, even called from Virginia Beach and said she was thinking the same way.

Psalms 91: 11-12
"For He will give His angels charge concerning you
To guard you in all your ways.
They will bear you up in their hands
That you do not strike your foot against a stone.

Sometime during those first few days I heard that Em, Gene's wingman, had made radio contact with Gene. Em went in search for Gene's plane and searched until he

was nearly out of fuel and was ordered back to the ship. He went back, refueled and then searched again. I was thankful for another glimmer of hope.

Two summers before - when Gene had a stretch of time at home, a few of my Bible Study friends and I had the opportunity to go to Washington DC to not only hear but to be with Corrie Ten Boom. Gene really wanted me to go and looked forward to having time alone with the children so I went. We had such an enlightening time. The meetings where she spoke at International Fellowship House were uplifting but the five of us had the rare privilege of going to the home where she stayed. We had an elegant dinner and then sat at her feet in the living room while she told stories. One that impressed me was when she and her frail sister, Betsie, were standing in line at Ravensbruck, the concentration camp. Guards were on either side of the long single file line going to the bathhouse. Corrie had hidden Betsie's medicine and a Bible in her undergarments. Corrie prayed, "Lord, cause now thine angels to surround me; and let them not be transparent today, for the guards must not see me." Calmly she passed the guards. Everyone was checked from the front, sides and back. The woman in front of her was checked. They let Corrie pass for they did not see her and Betsie right behind her, was checked. The same thing happened when they left the bathhouse.

When I got home I couldn't wait to tell Gene everything she said. We were sitting on the love seat and when I got to the part about the angels, I was on my knees beside him with my face in his and said "Isn't that exciting?!" He patted me and laughingly agreed.

Mom's neighbors, Pauline and Gordon, were so good to us - they stopped in every day, sometimes more than once. Pauline and I had been girlhood friends. Gordon was so good with the children and they grew to love him. He owned antique cars and quite often brought his Model T, Miss Abigail, up for them to ride in. How they enjoyed that! Gordon came to me one day and said he had found a go-cart for sale and I agreed that this was probably just the right time for them to have one (if it didn't have too much power). Gordon took the children to look it over and they came home with a not-so-new go-cart. Mom's

Miss Abigail

lovely oversized lawn was a go-cart track that summer but the children had a great time. Poor Gordon spent much time repairing it with four helpers watching every move he made. What good lessons they learned and what wonderful times they had together.

A personal help to me was my best friend, Molly. We had been like sisters since we were thirteen. We truly were kindred spirits in the way we loved Jesus and wanted to serve Him. Later we loved our husbands and children the same way. Molly didn't have to talk to comfort me - it was all in her eyes. She knew and loved Gene like a brother and I knew her loving prayers would sustain both of us. Looking back - I am certain that Molly was part of God's plan for my life. He gave us each other in order that we might be an influence for good in each other's lives - oh, that all girls could experience a friendship like that. Thank You, Lord, for the beautiful blessing of Molly in my life.

Bruce on the go cart

69

We stayed with Mom for six weeks and as the time drew closer for us to leave, I could sense her dejection. I knew that she was surrounded by faithful family members, a loving minister and loyal, helpful neighbors and friends; but she kept saying that they couldn't take our place. If she hadn't been a schoolteacher, I would have taken her home with me but we all had to get on with our lives. I feared she wouldn't eat properly so I prepared dinner packets for her to take from the freezer and pop in the oven. It was extremely hard to leave her.

The wound was opened again when we arrived in Virginia Beach. Happy as we were to be home and joyful as the children were as they bounded about from their rooms to the garage to get their bikes and take a quick ride to say "Hi" to neighborhood friends, I was finding it hard to see the tearful reminders of Gene throughout the house: his chair at the kitchen table, his workbench and tools in the garage, his slippers by our bed, his closet of civilian clothes, his extra toothbrush hanging near mine, his dresser, his books and our bed.

Friends started coming the first day - what a blessing they were! Reidun and Michelle came over and we realized that our relationship had grown from a friendship to a kinship - we were bonded together by our mutual loss. She didn't share the confidence that the Lord had given me and I tried to encourage her but the factual news was not good. By this time we had been informed that the plane was on fire, had crashed and exploded and no parachutes were seen. Our husbands remained Missing in Action. Even then my faith held strong. Thank you, Lord!

We couldn't wait for Sunday to come so we could worship with our church family. I was not going to start working again with the three choirs until September. Just arriving at church was overwhelming - our friends were so dear, so concerned and so wonderful. In the best of times it is very hard for me to hold tears back. One of the most priceless gifts (or fruits) that God gave me is a heart full of love - it just spills over all of the time, and seeing those radiant faces again almost did me in! After the service began everything spoke to me about Gene, so the poor children had to sit there and put up with their

Mom using tissue after tissue (and that is another reason I love them so much - they weren't ashamed - they just nestled in closer). Difficult as it was to go to church, there was something refreshing and cleansing about the release of those feelings. I am sorry it had to be done there but I was among people who understood me and after a few weeks I began to improve.

At first I cried at some time every day and then it turned to weeping. As the weeks went by, I could go longer periods without tears but it didn't take much to trigger them. My weekly trip to the commissary at Oceana was not easy because the roar of the jets and their saucy turns in the sky always struck a nerve.

We need to grieve and we need to cry - those are the times the Lord can comfort us best and when those times are over we feel refreshed and have renewed strength to go on. Gradually as we put our trust in Him and find our hope in Him we begin to realize in a way we never could before that He is the source of our strength. As we experience each added drop of His grace and mercy our hearts are filled with a fresh awareness of peace and thanksgiving because He cares and watches over us.

Soon after the children and I returned to Virginia Beach we were eating dinner at the table in the bay window dining nook of our kitchen and someone knocked on the door that went from the family room to the garage. No one ever came through the double garage to that door - everyone came to our double front doors or the sliding glass door in the family room, or the sliding glass door in the dining room. An unspoken sense of alarm came over us as I looked at the children and got up to go to the door. They were right behind me for protection. Bruce, then Thomas, then Mark and then Susan. I opened the door to see a black man standing at the foot of the steps. His kindly expression put us all at ease and I went down the steps asking if I could help him. He spoke haltingly and I could tell it had not been easy for him to come and knock on our door. He told me that "We uns jes want you to know that we heard about your husband and we want you to know that we think he is the finest white man we ever knew." His eyes were so sincere and showed such concern that my heart melted. I took his hand and thanked him so much for

71

coming to tell us that. He then asked if there was anything they could do and I told him they could pray and he said "I'm not much of a praying man but if you want me to pray, I will." And the tears fell down his cheeks. He told me that the other people in his community were praying people and he would tell them. He also said they would be "watching out" for us. The children and I were very moved by his visit and appreciated it more than he will ever know.

We lived on the corner of Edinburgh Drive (a woodsy secluded street) and Little Neck Road which was not a big highway but it was an access road to the elementary school and all sections across the road and to the back of us. One of those sections across the road had been there for many years before suburbia came near them; and that was where the man lived. One older man would walk by on Little Neck Road nearly everyday. We all waved and spoke to him but if Gene was home he would stop the man to visit. They talked about many things but Gene generally asked how the area used to be and he loved to talk about that. Gene really enjoyed talking to him and the other people that walked by.

The day that Gene's belongings arrived from the ship was not an easy one. I told the truck driver to put the cruise boxes in the garage and I would unpack them from there. The minute I opened them I was overcome by the "ship smell" that I had become so familiar with over the years. Memories and longings came over me as I knelt beside the cruise box, picked up one of his uniforms, hugged it to my heart and cried. After awhile I neatly placed it back in the box, closed the cruise boxes and decided to unpack them someday when I felt stronger.

We made a few of our special trips to the beach before that summer ended. The children had their wonderful zest for living back and it was good to be a part of their lives. Our bond was stronger now and we had the addition of a new feeling of protectiveness for each other. A determination had come over me also. I asked the Lord to help me be the same girl Gene left. I knew that if I allowed hatred and bitterness to creep in I wouldn't be the same so I asked to be filled with love and compassion.

72

September came and the children were eager to go back to school. When we did the school shopping I couldn't believe how they had grown! It was good to have all of our activities begin again. Bible Study was the greatest help to me and getting together with the choir again was like meeting with best friends. I started meeting with a group of POW MIA wives - there were 27 of us in the area and they were very special women. I liked them immediately but had no idea I would grow to love them as I did.

It was good for me to join the POW MIA wives group and be made more aware of the situation we were in. I already knew the policy of the US Government and had talked to the squadron officers wives about it as well as our family in Pennsylvania. The policy was that we were to remain silent about the POW MIA issue because we feared retaliation against the men. That fall of '68 we became more encouraged as the Paris Peace talks seemed closer to getting underway. Quite regularly we went to NAS Oceana to be briefed by men from the State Department and Navy Intelligence. As we got involved it seemed to lift our spirits to be doing something for our men. We began to believe that we needed to speak out. It seemed logical to us that if we could get Congress to move in that direction, the American public would stand behind us and the Vietnamese would be swayed by public opinion. Some of us started going to Washington monthly to knock on Congressmen and Senators doors. We were a part of the formation of the National League of Families of American Prisoners in Southeast Asia. Henry Kissinger met with us often to keep us informed about the Paris Peace Talks. Vice President Agnew met with us, President Nixon spoke to us and Senator Bob Dole gave us a great deal of support. In November 1968 the Paris Peace talks began - after a year of discussing preconditions such as location, attendees and even the shape of the table.

In early December the USS America came home. In a Navy town the homecoming of one of its ships is always highly covered by the local television news channels. I had not intended to watch the ship's arrival because it always made me cry; tears of sadness when they departed and tears of

73

joy as they returned. On this particular day the news was on while I was working in the kitchen. When I overheard her name - USS America - I was magnetized to stand in the doorway of the family room. Seeing the mighty vessel coming in to dock with the men standing at parade rest at extended intervals the full length of the flight deck and watching the wives and children, the mothers and dads and sweethearts waving, jumping to be seen, calling or holding placards of welcome, pulls at your heart. But when you experience the relief that comes to them as the men file down the gangway, hurry to meet their loved ones and at long last melt into each other's arms - you really can't hold back your tears of joy for them. Lost in their happiness I quickly came back to reality. My tears were for Gene as I returned to the kitchen. How I missed him and loved him and longed to hear from him. How I yearned to stand before him with his arms around me so I could rest my head on his chest under his chin and feel his heartbeat and hear his breathing. How long would it be? Thank You Lord for keeping Gene fresh in my mind and thank You for giving me patience - please give me more.

I knew it would be hard when the squadron came home. It was not that I resented the other men for returning, on the contrary, I had been praying for their safe return. During their time in Vietnam, one more plane had been shot down. I was relieved when their tour was over. When they came to call on me I was really touched to see and know how much they loved and respected Gene. His shoot down had been very hard on all of them. I appreciated listening to them as they reminisced and told little stories. I was grateful to know that every Saturday night Gene made his rounds to knock on their doors and remind them that Chapel would be held the following morning. They were a great comfort to me and I was thankful they were with their families again. The Lord had lifted me over another hurdle and now I could close that chapter of my life.

74

THE PATCHWORK of MY LIFE

Chapter 12

Mom

Friends brought Mom for a weekend in early October and then the children and I went home for Thanksgiving. I was concerned because she had lost so much weight but when I talked to her about it she said she was not hungry and just did not want to eat. If I prepared the food she ate well but when I was gone she only smoked and drank coffee.

Those years really took their toll on Mom. Before Dad's stroke her life had been wonderful. Mom was very intelligent. She was valedictorian of her large high school class and had gone to Elmira College. In all, she had studied Spanish for nine years and even worked in Washington DC one summer teaching Spanish immigrants how to speak English. She was a tall (5'10"), stately, attractive woman who carried her height with dignity and charm. Whatever she did, she did wholeheartedly. She was the perfect hostess and was noted for her hospitality. She and Dad had a rare marriage - she loved him heart and soul and he treated her like a queen on a pedestal. She could be feisty and no one could ever cross her; but Dad was gentle and good-natured and always knew how to soften her. He admittedly "babied" her by bringing her flowers and showering her with gifts even when times were hard (we started out during the depression) and he took her dancing every Friday night. They worked hard together but also knew how to relax and enjoy life. We had a cottage on Keuka Lake (one of New York's Finger Lakes) where we spent part of each summer and many weekends throughout the year. When Jim was old enough to start school, she started teaching and she was a gifted teacher - the accolades she received over the years were countless - from loving, appreciative students and parents and also from

the administration. But better than that she was a wonderful mother and Jim and I loved her.

Needless to say, it was difficult to see her life change. She put up a good front in her work-a-day life but the nagging depression was inside her to wear her down. When Jim died it became even worse and then Dad's death brought her down even further. When Gene was shot down she rallied to protect me but within a short time it was even harder for her because my situation was unique and all eyes turned toward me. I was sensitive to her needs and tried to be on guard to direct some of the attention to her.

Mom had not wanted us to leave her during the summer but I had hoped that she would grow stronger and more independent when she started teaching again. It seemed best (and I had prayed about it) for us to return to our life in Virginia Beach. The children were well adjusted to our community of school, church, friends and activities. I felt a strong need to be where Gene expected me to be in case of some miraculous escape (I can dream can't I?) and Virginia Beach was a hub where I could keep abreast of all the information about Gene that I hungered for. More than ever I needed my church, Bible Study, choir and friends. Because that summer of '68 was such an upsetting time, I couldn't even imagine going through all that would be required of us to move from Virginia Beach to Pennsylvania - it just didn't seem like the right time to make such a drastic change in our lives. But I knew that my decision to stay in Virginia Beach was part of Mom's problem - if I stayed with her and cooked for her she would eat. It was a great concern to me.

When Mom came to be with us for the Christmas holiday I was terribly worried about her. She was extremely thin and her complexion was a chalky gray when we picked her up at the airport. That evening we had the caroling party and she enjoyed it but after everyone left she told me that she had TB. She said that she had tested positive when they did the routine school testing. I expressed my concern about her being around her school children but she had just been notified a few days earlier and nothing had been said about her teaching yet. She had gone for a chest x-ray and it was confirmed there was a spot on her lung. She would be going in for further tests the Wednesday after school started again and if it was worse they would hospitalize her. I phoned all of the people that had come to the party to tell them they should be tested - just in case anyone had been exposed and the children and I were tested also.

After the cantata, family Christmas and Mom's return to Pennsylvania, I talked with all my Christian friends whom I hadn't already told about Mom, expressing my deep concern and asking everyone to pray for Mom. We had studied James in Sunday School and I kept re-reading the verses in Chapter 5 about prayer:

James 5: 14-15

Is anyone among you sick? Then he must call for the elders of the church and they are to pray over him, anointing him with oil in the name of the Lord and the prayers offered in faith will restore the one who is sick and the Lord will raise him up and if he has committed sins, they will be forgiven him.

Many people were praying for Mom and I started praying for it to go away. I just wanted Mom to get better and I didn't see how she could handle this added burden. Our minister talked to me and said he would like to do an anointing using me as Mom's representative. I had never experienced anything like that but felt comfortable with the dear Christian friends he invited to participate. We met near the altar in our church and as we prayed in sincere faith, he touched my forehead with oil. We all left the church with a confidence that God had answered our prayers. I called Mom after her appointment on Wednesday and she sounded the best I had heard her sound in months. She told me that the doctor was very puzzled - the spot was gone! I told her about our prayers and she was very thankful.

I took the opportunity to talk to her about smoking - something I hadn't done in over twenty years (I had told her when I was in college that I loved her and respected her but I wished she did not smoke). I asked her what the doctor said about her smoking and she said that he told her smoking had nothing (???) to do with her illness and she added, "While I was waiting for the results of the x-ray his nurse came out

and had a cigarette with me." What could I say? I just prayed about it!

My birthday is April 15th and this was an exciting one. I was forty that spring of 1969 and when Mom called to wish me a Happy Birthday she said she was giving me a present I would never see. When I asked, "What is it?" she told me she had smoked her last cigarette and she would never smoke again. I was ecstatic - she never gave me a better present! I was so proud of her and loved her so much! She had smoked for forty-two years and I realized how hard this was for her. Her health improved and she was happier.

Thank you Lord Jesus for Your miraculous answer to prayer!

Chapter 13

Rejoice? Rejoice!!

1969 was not the best year of my life. Even now as I look back on it I am filled with a gnawing heartache. I recall the day in, day out sprints to the mailbox, heart pounding with anticipation, hoping for word about Gene or (glory be!) that I might find a letter from him. Other wives received mail and my silent hope continued week after week and month after month.

I poured myself into the life our children and I had and was always aware of the strength and encouragement that I received from my Lord and Savior. I always was at rest in His loving-kindness and felt the protection of being under the shadow of His wings but something was lacking and I needed to whole-heartedly turn to Him for help again. I needed to "gain new strength, mount up with wings like eagles, run and not grow tired, walk and not become weary." (Isaiah 40:31) I was so thankful for the strength I gleaned from His word in the Bible —there was always something new to enlighten me.

Soon after Gene's accident I received a card with a poem about how to walk down the road of life. It stated that if you walk with God, no matter what comes your way, you will walk down the pathway of life rejoicing every step of the way. That word rejoicing was a real stumbling block to me. I felt at peace, I never doubted - never once did I say, "Why, Lord?" and I truly felt His presence - but rejoice?!

It troubled me that this poem inferred that my walk was not quite in tune. I turned to the Bible and found consolation in Romans 12:12 "Rejoicing in hope, patient in tribulation and continuing instant in prayer." I thanked the Lord for that verse - for the hope He gave me, for giving me patience

80

during a time of tribulation and I was continuing instant in prayer.

"Rejoicing" - could that be the ingredient that was lacking in my life? I needed to pray about it!

The children and I looked forward to summer vacation when we would spend a few weeks with Mom. They wanted to tune up the go-cart, get the engine started, rev it up and make their continuous journey around the circular track. We decided to make the track in the flat part of the pasture this year in order that Grammy's lawn wouldn't be damaged again. Bruce was going to work for a local farmer. Thomas was going to mow and care for Grammy's lawn, Mark and Susan would be taking swimming lessons at the pool in Troy and I needed to do a lot of cleaning at the home we owned in Pennsylvania.

The plans helped us get through the remainder of spring. Though we were all busy we were finding it hard to keep a "stiff upper lip." Something was missing from our lives and we needed a lift. Fortunately May is a good beach month and we were able to go a few times in the afternoon after school, and as we had done in past years we picked strawberries at a nearby strawberry farm and prepared some of them for the freezer.

There were times during that first year that I realized the worst could happen. I was learning through The National League of Families that some men died in the crash or only a few days after capture and some had died during internment. I needed proof that Gene was alive because I felt that once I had confirmation from the North Vietnamese that they were holding him - then they would have to give an accounting for him when the conflict was over. I worked and prayed for that breakthrough.

I knew in my heart that Gene was alive and I was still grateful, beyond words, for that faith but little things were happening to make me almost desperate for proof. After church one Sunday we were in the car, leaving the parking lot, when Susan got off her seat and was standing on the floor behind me (this was before seatbelts). She wrapped her arms around my neck and put her head on my shoulder. I asked her what was wrong as I patted her head and she told me a boy in her

Sunday School class had told her that her Daddy was dead. Susan said, "He isn't, my Mommy knows it!" but the boy told her that his Mommy and Daddy said "Your Mommy is crazy." I stopped the car and Bruce, Thomas, & Mark helped her over the back of the seat and into my arms where I could engulf her with love. We all comforted her and reaffirmed our belief. We prayed for that family and asked the Lord to confirm our faith to others.

(I continued to pray for the family and about a year later while I was ironing one Saturday, I was overcome by a strong feeling to pray specifically for them - so I prayed! The very next morning in church she came to me with eyes aglow and told me they were talking with a gentleman the afternoon before and the subject turned to one about the need for salvation. She and her husband both accepted Christ! Isn't He wonderful the way He impresses a need on our hearts in order that we may share in the joy even though we are a very small part of His wonderful plan to bring more people into His family?!)

We were beginning to see some accomplishment from our efforts with the POW & MIA situation and I can best share that with you by letting you read the letter I sent to our friends in October 1969.

October 1969

Dear Friend:

Even though this is a form letter please take it personally because I have already made up my mailing list and I think of you individually as I write. So many have asked and are concerned about Gene that I want to use this means to update you.

First of all, let me thank you for your prayers. I know Gene has been strengthened by them. They also have sustained the children and me. The Lord has blessed us and I am, indeed, thankful to have such wonderful friends.

Many of you have not heard from me since last Christmas. I know you wonder about Gene and yet you hesitate to

ask - I understand how you must feel. We have not had a word - no letter from him and no release of his name from Hanoi. I write to him each month on a six-line form but it is quite doubtful that he has ever been given one of my letters. The released prisoners told me that for each letter they were allowed to write they were given one from their family. Since Gene has never been able to write he, most likely, has never received one.

When you have asked me "What can I do?" I have always answered "Pray!" I surely want you to continue doing that but now I am ready to ask you to do even more. Things have changed and I'll try to explain it as best I can.

For nearly five years it was the official United States position to treat the Prisoner of War and Missing in Action matter with caution, in the hope that the North Vietnamese would alter their P.O.W. policy. They (U.S.) felt the quiet approach would produce the best results. When it seemed unproductive they changed tactics - starting with Secretary Laird's press conference last May. He pointed out that North Vietnam was not abiding by the standards set up in the Geneva Convention which they agreed to on 5 June 1957.

In August Lt. Bob Frishman and P.O. Doug Hegdahl were released from a prison camp in Hanoi. After they returned officials said that continued silence for fear of retaliation might be interpreted by Hanoi as government passiveness on the prisoner issue. They said that all diplomatic effort to get better treatment of P.O.W.'s have failed. So - on 2 Sept. 1969 Bob Frishman and Doug Hegdahl spoke out and told the world that the treatment was not humane.

Now it is firmly believed that public opinion will sway Hanoi! Recently a number of us went to Washington. It was gratifying to hear our Representatives resolve to uphold our husbands or sons. They, too, feel that public opinion will accomplish what we want. This was proven when in early 1967 Hanoi stated they would try U. S. Pilots as criminals —murderers! The world was appalled and let it be known - Ho Chi Minh backed down.

I belong to a very active organization. It is the "National League of Families of American Prisoners in Southeast Asia." Within the last few months we have climbed over

83

our wall of secrecy and have started our own crusade. Many of these families have publicized their husband or son. There are a number of my friends here in Virginia Beach that have told their husbands' story on T.V., radio or in the newspaper. Some of us, however, are still reluctant to give out information of our husbands for publication. We fear that something we might say would cause him further persecution as we know local Communists are watching for such material so they can send it on to Hanoi.

As you have assumed I fall in this latter category. I don't want Gene's story told but much can be done without giving a run-down on him. This is where I call on you. The key to this whole campaign is public opinion and how can we get that? We have made up a packet and I am enclosing one for you. After you have read it you will realize that letters will get the public opinion we need. I believe that each of you (and I'm sending out 200 of these) can:

1. Write a least five letters for me to those indicated in the packet.

2. Ask as many of your friends and relatives to do this as you possibly can.

3. Talk to your clergyman about Nov. 8th or 9th (whichever is your day of worship) and encourage him to urge his congregation to write.

I know you will do this for Gene. Can you imagine the magnitude of these letters? If it is public opinion that is needed - we can do it - can't we?! Faith can move mountains and our letters will open the doors for the ultimate release of our Prisoners of War.

Always remember not to write abusive letters. Uphold our wonderful country and our government. Place the blame for this sad situation where it belongs - on the North Vietnamese government.

Gene is outstanding among men. He is compassionate, unselfish and genuinely concerned for others. He has unlimited inner strength and this comes from his close relation with his Lord. He is proud to be an American and has served his country well. He is far more than my inadequate words can express for he fills my heart. How thankful I am that God made us one.

I am ready to plead for his freedom. Won't you please help me and support him with your loyalty and concern?

I'll never be able to thank you enough!

Your loving friend,
Jeanne

I continued to work and pray for a break-through concerning Gene and it came two days before Christmas (eighteen months after he was shot down). The children and I received a beautiful message from him. It was a radio broadcast and first came over NBC news and though we did not actually hear it, some of our friends heard it and let us know. We were overjoyed and very thankful!

The next evening was Christmas Eve. Mom had come to spend her vacation with us. After dinner our Postmaster came to the door with a stack of late mail. I thought it was unusual to have an evening delivery and such personal service but he said he was on his way

home and thought I might like the rest of my cards before Christmas. I sat down in the family room (where Mom was reading the paper) and with the stack of mail in my lap I started opening and reading them one by one. When I came to the last one - it looked strange to me with foreign printing and then I recognized Gene's writing. My heart was pounding as I opened and read the six-line letter.

I looked at Mom and said, "Gene has had a stroke." Suddenly the

After our first letter
from Gene
Christmas 1969

children were in the room and the whole house was in an uproar - hugging, reading the letter, dancing from room to room - just going crazy!!

Later we had to go to church for a late night Christmas Eve Cantata. You can't believe the outpouring of love and thanksgiving in that church that night. Prayers had been answered and everyone was jubilant to have proof that Gene was alive.

Oh, precious Lord, thank You for this beautiful confirmation! Thank You even more that You gave me proof eighteen months ago when You assured me that Gene was alive!!

I really don't know as I look at that letter now, why I said, "Gene has had a stroke", so quickly and emphatically - other than God allowed me to have that insight while I was reading it. His writing seemed methodical and carefully precise whereas in the past it was freely flowing. Of course he hadn't held a pen in eighteen months but still there was something different. We had to send our letters on to the Bureau of Naval Personnel soon after we received them. When I sent mine (with some reluctance- his hands had been on that paper!), I told them of my supposition and sent an old letter that Gene had written to me and when they compared them they concurred that I might be right. I didn't actually know that Gene had a stroke until he came home and told me.

Our Christmas was a joyous day. Friends who heard about the radio message were calling from far and near to express their thanksgiving. We in turn were able to share our letter with them and all in all it made for a happy day. The children and I felt a noticeable relief and we were pleased that Mom was there to enjoy the blessed day and share in all of our excitement. The whole week turned into a celebration with friends stopping in to express their feelings with us. All too quickly Mom's holiday was over and we had to take her to the airport for her return trip to her home in Pennsylvania.

Within a day or two after Christmas the written form of the radio message arrived from Navy Intelligence which gave us even more reason to celebrate. It follows:

86

NOW FOR A CHRISTMAS MESSAGE SENT HOME
FROM CDR. WALTER WILBER A U.S. PILOT CAPTURED
IN THE DEMOCRATIC REPUBLIC OF VIETNAM.

TO: Mrs. Walter E. Wilber
3212 Edinburgh Dr.
Virginia Beach, Virginia

Dearest Jeanne and Bruce, Thomas, Mark and Susan:

As the Blessed Christmas Day approaches I want you to know these things: I love you and miss you very much. You are always in my thoughts and prayers and I am safe, healthy and strong. Do not give any worry about me as I am just fine. My living conditions are good and my hopes are higher. I trust your health is equally as good. Please take special good care of yourself. Spare no expense whatever regarding your health, education and welfare so you may enjoy the fullest meaning of Christ birth each day of the year.

Children I feel that you have continued to be good and helpful to your mother, therefore, I know Santa Claus will not forget you. Thank you for the Christmas present last year and I am hoping for another package soon. Blessed family I love you, please work hard and pray incessantly for peace on Earth, especially Christmas Eve.

MERRY CHRISTMAS!
ALL MY LOVE,
DADDY

As soon as Gene's name was released I started speaking. The people were hungry to hear about our efforts and very anxious to be given something to do for the POW & MIA's so we had requests coming in every day. I spoke for Navy wives groups, Bible Studies, church groups, Lions, Rotary (and other service clubs), Veterans, schools and even groups of women that would gather together in one of their neighborhood homes. We were there to tell them about the Prisoner issue, our organization, share our own story and give out information about writing letters. I never dreamed everyone would be so eager to help.

87

I was also writing letters to everyone I could think of that might be able to spread the message for us. I even wrote to "Dear Abby" because I knew that her newspaper column reached nearly every home in the United States, but she wrote back and said "the issue did not interest or apply to the general public." This is what I had written to her:

March 1970

Dear Abby,

You listen to the problems of people from all walks of life. I admire you for hearing and commend you for the sound advice that you give. Perhaps you would be kind enough to help me.

My problem is not one similar to those I read in your column. I am thankful I have never had to cope with many of their anxieties and my heart goes out to them.

I am aware of my blessings - my four children (two of whom are teenagers) are obedient, loving and considerate. My friends are loyal. I have always found associates and even strangers to be warm and friendly. It is a privilege to be a member of this American family.

My husband is, without question, the most wonderful man I have ever known. I stand in grateful awe that he chose me to be his wife and the mother of his children. We have always been aware that the Lord blessed our union.

So what is my problem?

Why have I turned to you?

My husband is a Prisoner of War in North Vietnam. I could write pages about the barbaric treatment of the prisoners, the mental anguish of many wives, children and parents and the unfulfilled promises of the North Vietnamese but I realize you haven't the space or time.

We wives have one single aim and that unites us in a very close bond. We want release for our men. For months we have been working our hearts out. We speak, we travel to reach new people, we plead for humane treatment and we have begged for the public opinion that is required but we still go to bed weary and frus-

trated for we can't see enough accomplishment - we can't see the end. We fear for our husband's mentality, his physical well-being and his life. We want so much to help him and yet we can't speak loudly enough - we can't reach every heart in America. We fear our husbands might be forgotten as the Prisoner of War issue is pushed to the background and almost ignored.

We feel it is time for the men of this nation to take a stand on the prisoner issue. Must the wives and families of these men, who have already given so much, carry the standard alone? Our American Heritage is rich and proud. Have the principles of this nation degenerated to the extent that no one is willing to take a firm stand?

In past wars we have all felt indebted to the men who fought for our country. We have sent them off undergirded with our genuine expressions of pride and support. We have kept them ever in mind on the home front and have sustained them with our allegiance. We have shed tears when Old Glory passed by fluttering against a blue sky and symbolized to us the dedication of our forefathers, the bravery of our fighting men defending our beloved nation, the blessedness of freedom, the unity of our people and the promises of the future.

Have times changed so? No - our men are still going off to war and their families still have the same old feelings. Have the rest of us just grown a little reserved perhaps - afraid to let the world know that we still feel a responsibility beyond our immediate home or community - that we still hold a deep appreciation for our fellow man? I beg all Americans to break loose from apathy, breathe deeply the exhilaration of "doing," smell the sweet aroma of concern, open your eyes to the promises of the future and let us all strive in every way to work toward a truly United States of America.

The problems of the nation are the problems of its people. The prisoners of war issue is a problem and it is everyone's responsibility. Won't you - every single one of you - let your congressman know that you are concerned for our Prisoners of War and urge him to take immediate action in working out a program for release?

Don't be afraid to support men like Ross Perot whose unselfish aim is to free these men. We need public opinion. Please let the world know that you care. I implore you to take

a firm stand now so that you may be instrumental in the release of our men - each one of whom would give his life for America. Can we do less than support them with our loyalty and concern?

Some of the wives have been wondering for five years whether they are a wife or a widow. My story isn't near that sad but I long to see him again that I might care for him and comfort him. I want him home so our children can know the priceless privilege of growing under his guidance and direction.

Will you please help me?

I will be forever grateful!

Jeanne Wilber - a POW wife

After mid-January I began to feel the let down from the exhilaration that I had experienced at Christmas time. By mid February I was resenting the fact that the North Vietnamese had made us wait for eighteen months when they could have notified our government the very day he was shot down. My trips to the mailbox were more frequent and filled with far more anxiety than they had been through 1969 - they had promised one letter each month. Through March I was still speaking, directing the choirs and doing all the other things I was involved in - we were having a Bible Study in our home on Sunday evenings but my heart was getting heavier.

In the first week of April - two years after Gene left - I took time out to analyze myself again and I realized how much I needed the Lord's help. I was close to Him and I prayed for Gene, the children, Mom, a sick friend, a new baby - everyone but me again. I prayed long into the night and felt so relieved when I turned it all over to Him. The next morning I woke up and felt jubilant! My heart was pounding with excitement and all I could think was "Expect a miracle!" Those three words kept going over and over in my mind. I couldn't wait to go to my Bible Study class that morning and share it with the girls.

90

That was April 7th and on April 15th another message was released from a Prisoner of War. It was a birthday message to me from Gene. I had never heard of a prisoner

After our second message from Gene - April 1970

sending a birthday message prior to that. Four days later at 11 o'clock Sunday night my phone rang. It was a man from an anti-war group. He said he was in San Francisco - he had just arrived there from Hanoi where he had met with three prisoners and one was my husband. He even took a picture of Gene and told me he would send it to me.

To me these were miracles but greater than that again was the fact that He gave me the hope I needed ahead of time. He gave me the joy eight days before my miracle of Gene's message actually happened. Isn't He wonderful? He taught me to rejoice in hope.

That night when I was praying I was trying to thank Him for this feeling. My cup and my eyes were overflowing as I counted all my blessings. Normally I pray myself to sleep but that night I had to turn my light back on and open my Bible again. It opened to Psalms 5:11: "But let all those that put their trust in Thee rejoice, let them ever shout for joy, because Thou defendest them, let them also that love Thy name be joyful in Thee."

91

Chapter 14

The Big Move

We received our second letter from Gene in April also and in it Gene asked me to sell or rent our home in Virginia Beach. That meant he wanted us to move to our farm in Pennsylvania. It came as a surprise to us and it gave us a great deal to think about but Bruce had an immediate reaction. He was sixteen, would be a senior in September and had the best friends he had ever had. We had lived there for six years - the longest we had ever lived any place and we had put in deep roots. After Bruce was able to think it over he suggested that the rest of us move to Pennsylvania and he would move in with his best friend. I dismissed it by saying, "We are a family and can not be separated - if you don't feel right about leaving now - none of us will." I knew that if I insisted Bruce would go because he was obedient but I did not want to force him to give up everything to move to Pennsylvania and then not be able to make a good adjustment. His happiness was very precious to me and Gene would understand if we waited another year until after Bruce had graduated from high school.

I started praying about it because I did want to do what the Lord and Gene wanted us to do. We were all comfortable there - each child had very special friends, our neighborhood was ideal and when Gene left he had been president of the Men's Club in our church so those men felt a real responsibility to our children. They treated them like their very own. They came to our house to help the boys clean out our rain gutters, rake the lawn or do general maintenance and repair work. They also took them to ball games and other local events. I can't begin to list my attachments there - they were far too numerous and far too heartfelt. Not only was my love for the countless friends from every

walk of life so great that it almost stifled me when I allowed myself to think of leaving them. But also it was Gene - this is where we lived together and where my memories of him were so vivid - how could I close that door behind me? The Lord would have to change our hearts if He wanted us to leave Virginia Beach!

In May I started taking the three younger children to the beach after school. Thomas and Mark started talking about life on the farm and planning how they would arrange their bedroom. Susan began making her plans about the little room that would be hers with the soft colored roses on the wallpaper and the view of Saxton's Knob from her window. As they talked and as we planned together our excitement grew and our life began to take on a new feeling of adventure. I was pleased to see how the Lord was working in our lives but I didn't say anything to Bruce. I just kept praying.

In early June my Mom called late one night and told me our home in Pennsylvania had been broken into. The robbers had broken a window and two door jams and taken quite a few things. My main concern was Mom - she was upset about it. My cousin was a contractor so I asked Mom to call and have him make the necessary repairs and seal the house back up again.

I prayed long into the night - by now I knew I did not want to burden Mom with the responsibility of watching over our home but I still couldn't move unless Bruce was agreeable. I left it with Jesus that night - but if we were to move I wanted Bruce to tell me - I needed to know it was all right with him.

The next morning while we were eating breakfast I told the children about my conversation with Grammy. I just stated the facts and did not try to do any persuading. That afternoon when Bruce came home from school I was in the garage so I walked out to greet him. He didn't even say "Hi" - he just looked down (he was 6'2") and said, "If Dad wants us to move and you think we should - then we'd better do it!!" I hugged him and said he was my answer to prayer. He laughed and said, "I knew you were praying Mom. I couldn't even concentrate in school this morning cuz I kept getting all these thoughts about moving."

Thomas, Mark and Susan took the news with great enthusiasm and Bruce seemed to be enjoying the fact that he was responsible for causing all of the happiness in the family. When you stop to think about it, only the Lord could be given credit for the way our mindset completely reversed. It is comforting to know that He will guide and direct you if you will just let Him have control. Suddenly we realized how much we had to do in order to move but we could get it done through the summer with His help. I continued to pray for His guidance, direction and the working out of so many details. We had a big job ahead!

In church on Sunday I shared my news with the choir, asked them to pray for us and told them my biggest concern right then was to know what to do about selling or renting our home. When we arrived home after church the phone was ringing. It was a friend from California who had been in one of Gene's squadrons. He told me they had just received orders to the Norfolk area and they would like to rent in Virginia Beach. He wondered if I would track down some listings and send them the information. When I told him about Gene's letter and the decision we had just made, he said, "I'll take it! We would love to rent your house sight unseen! Can we move in on July 1st?"

If Jesus can provide a renter for our home in one hour I am sure He can help us move in 2-1/2 weeks!!

Monday I went to the base to make arrangements for our move on June 30th (Mark's 10th birthday) and then I went back home to start painting windows. Bruce, Thomas and I had started painting our house that spring and there were still eight windows to paint. I painted every spare minute until they were finished. One big job that had to be done was to have our friends in Pennsylvania move all of the furnishings from our home up there to our barn so the house would be empty and ready for the Virginia Beach furniture.

Miraculously and I mean **Miraculously** (because you can not imagine the details that had to be worked out) we were on our way Home. We had a parakeet whose name was Pudgi and his cage was between me and whichever one of the

94

Painting our Virginia Beach home
Spring 1970

95

children was having their turn to ride up front. I loved to teach birds how to talk so Pudgi had an unbelievable vocabulary. The children counted over 500 words. During that fast forward period of time just prior to our move as I rushed by him or took the time to do a speedy cleaning of his cage I repeated the phrase, "Bruce, Tom, Mark and Susan - we're going to Pennsylvania!" Pudgi had a bell suspended by a chain from the top of the cage and he had complete control of that bell. If he wanted it to ring he would reach out and peck it and if he did not want it to ring he left it alone. Well - the motion of the car made the bell ring constantly and it nearly drove him crazy - it wasn't that he didn't like the sound of the ringing - he didn't like not being in control! He awkwardly stood on his perch and tried putting one foot on the bell but it would not hold still and he would lose his balance. He tried clinging to the side of the cage and catching it with his beak as it merrily jingled along. He bounded back on his perch and with broadened shoulders, feathers standing up on the back of his head and using all the authority he could muster he scolded then scolded some more; but it was all to no avail - the defiant bell kept ringing.

He couldn't talk - he couldn't eat or drink. He slouched in the corner for awhile as if to say, "This clanging bell is disturbing my happy home and ruining my trip!" As if enlightened by a brilliant idea he jumped back on his perch and stretching his neck as far as he could, he then got his head under the suspended bell and gently pulled himself back to a comfortable position on the perch with the bell on his head like a cap. The bell was silent! If parakeets could smile he would have grinned. Pudgi rode all the way home with the bell on his head proudly saying, "Bruce, Tom, Mark and Susan, we're going to Pennsylvania."

We laughed at that bird all day long. We were trying to make Mark's birthday a special day for him but Pudgi did the entertaining. Mark was such a joy to me - always caring, helpful and cheerful. Thank you, dear Lord, for giving me such an easy son to raise. Thank you for the comfort he always gives me. Bless him Lord - keep him in Your loving care!

 One of the other joys of June was another birthday message from Gene to Susan:

Here is a message home from Walter Eugene Wilber, Commander, U.S. Navy, U.S. Pilot captured in the democratic Republic of Vietnam:

(Here follows recording of a male voice speaking with an American accent-Ed) to Mrs. Walter Eugene Wilber, 3212 Edinburg Drive, Virginia Beach, Virginia 23452 twothreefourfivetwo, USA

From Walter Eugene Wilber, Commander, U.S. Navy, Camp of Detention for U.S. Pilots captured in Democratic Republic of Vietnam.

For Susan on June 2d second, 1970 Oneninesevenzero,

Happy Birthday, Susan, I think you must be such a big girl now that you are eight years old. Daddy always remembered you with those long, golden curls and big blue eyes. I can send you only my love and best wishes for happiness, good health and safety. Have a Happy Birthday. Enjoy your summer vacation so you can learn even better in the third grade. Although you are yet very young, pay attention to the principles Mommy teaches you from the Bible, and as you grow, faithfully follow them so you can pattern your life after your Mother. Tell your big brothers I love them. Always be our sweet Susan, and Happy Birthday.

Jeanne, I love you, be kind to yourselves and keep your heart full of love. My health is fine. Love to all, Gene, Daddy (Recording ends-Ed)

(Announcer-Ed) That was Commander Walter Eugene Wilber, U.S. Pilot captured in the Democratic Republic of Vietnam, addressing his daughter on the occasion of her birthday, 032300 ECC/Johnson EM 04/04552 JUN

At the same time we were trying to unpack and settle the house I had to be thinking about the furniture in the barn. The exposure would not be good for it so I called a local auctioneer and two weeks after we moved in we had an auction here (I can now say "here" because this is where we still live thirty-one years later). Such a busy time but such a wonderful summer! We never had hoped that we could love it so much here and be so happy. We bought a black Labrador puppy and named her

Beauty and we had a yellow kitten named Benjamin. Because they grew up together they loved each other. When they were little Beauty started picking Benjamin up in her mouth and she would walk all over with the kitten calmly hanging from the dog's mouth. They continued doing that when they were both full-sized animals. The children were happy to live where we could comfortably keep animals. We bought a John Deere lawn tractor because we had a large lawn. Gradually we got everything settled and made the house a home. Mom was on a cloud because she could drive over here every day and be with us. Bruce was accepted on the football team and started early practice with them. I was anxious to have a garden but the garden plot had not been cared for in twenty years so it was quite a struggle to get it started with only a hoe, rake and spade to work with. It was good exercise for me but most of all it was a solace. My very best times for talking to Jesus were in my garden and that is still true today.

Chapter 15

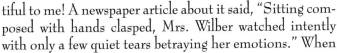

My Constant Plea

During the summer I started getting requests to speak but I wanted to spend my time with the children so I waited until they were in school. Once I started it seemed like a snowball and became even more demanding than my schedule had been in Virginia Beach.

Letters and messages were fairly regular all through 1970 and then at Christmas time Gene and another prisoner were going to be televised. We were notified on Saturday, December 26th that a fifteen-minute telecast would be aired on CBS and NBC sometime Sunday, December 27th (our eighteenth wedding anniversary) and that film crews would be arriving from Cleveland, New York City and Canada. Sunday afternoon they started arriving and you wouldn't believe the amount of equipment that was being carried in and installed in our family room. There were cameramen from CBS, NBC, CBC, API and local television crews and technicians. Our television receiver failed when I turned it on so I called a friend who was a TV repairman and he tried to fix it but wasn't completely satisfied so he and a neighbor brought in another set. The floodlights made the room so hot that we had the door wide open (which you never do during the cold winters of northern Pennsylvania). The phone rang constantly. I was concerned that everyone was hungry when we found out the telecast would not be on until 10:00 PM so I was in the kitchen preparing food for everyone. Finally we saw Gene. It was the first time the children and I had seen him move in 2-1/2 years. He looked beautiful to me! A newspaper article about it said, "Sitting composed with hands clasped, Mrs. Wilber watched intently with only a few quiet tears betraying her emotions." When

it was over the article stated that I said, "I felt drained." (I think most anyone would feel drained after a day like that)?! But I was happy I had seen Gene.

Gene had spoken out against the war and I was bombarded with questions about that. My answer was "I don't know his true feelings." The Defense Department called it "enemy propaganda." I truthfully was so starry eyed about watching him that the message did not affect me. I only knew that Gene was a loyal American and would never do or say anything that was not in the best interest of his country.

There was a great deal of media coverage the next day and then on Tuesday, December 29th this editorial was printed in the Elmira, NY Star Gazette:

Editorials

Mrs. Wilber Receives a Most Fitting 'Gift'

THE COLLECTIVE hearts of the Twin Tiers beat a little faster Sunday night - though none as fast as Mrs. Wilber and her four children. In deed, it is doubtful that anyone watching national television that night could not have been stirred by the films of Mrs. Wilber's husband, Navy Cmdr. W. Eugene Wilber, speaking from North Vietnam, where he has been held a prisoner of war for 2-1/2 years.

Commander Wilber and another Navy pilot were selected for the interview, which was filmed on Christmas Day by a Canadian TV newsman.

In the films, which were censored, the two prisoners said the war should be ended immediately.

This drew from a Defense Department spokesman a comment that the televised interview was an "enemy propaganda film."

Mrs. Wilber had no comment on that segment of the interview with her husband other than to say, "I don't know his true feelings."

She watched the telecast at the Wilbers' farmhouse at Coryland, near Columbia Cross Roads. With her were three of the Wilber children. A fourth was with friends in Virginia.

What Commander Wilber said about the war was not unexpected. But even the staunchest of "hawks" - and there doesn't seem to be very many of them left today - would be compassionate enough to wait until the joyful day when the Bradford County prisoner is released to learn whether he was speaking his sentiments fully when interviewed.

Neither was the Defense Department reaction a surprise. It rightly used the moment, also, to score the Hanoi government for not living up to its promises as a signer of the Geneva Convention by refusing impartial inspection and direct contact with the American POWs.

But for the time being Mrs. Wilber's heart has been relieved by seeing her husband on TV and knowing that he is well.

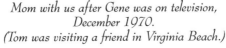

Mom with us after Gene was on television,
December 1970.
(Tom was visiting a friend in Virginia Beach.)

102

It was a fitting "gift" on the couple's 18th wedding anniversary - and with her other Twin Tier neighbors, we rejoice with her.

A few days after that I wrote this letter to the Editor:

Letters to the Editor
Thanks from the Wilbers

To the Editor:

I want to thank you for your most sincere concern for my husband (Navy Cmdr. W. Eugene Wilber, a North Vietnamese prisoner or war). The news coverage that you gave him last week made me very aware of your feelings. Not only have I been impressed by the reporters with whom it has been my pleasure to have contact, but also I want to express my gratitude for your editorial (Dec. 19). It proved again that hearts are compassionate.

It also drew me very close to the members of this community that Gene and I have always been proud to call "home." We are happy to share our joy with you and gratified that you rejoice with us.

The excitement of the telecast of my husband and the high pitch of interview are over. Life has found its regular pattern again but one small thing keeps my mind at unrest. Your last article was well written and I thank dear friends for all that was said but the children and I feel that there is so much more of Gene. We just want your readers to know the man he is - not the boy he was.

Gene is a devoted father. His tender love, high ideals and steadfast example are firmly imprinted in the children's hearts. Susan was only 5 when he left and now she is 8-1/2 but she remembers him well - his love is very real to her. The three boys are motivated by guidance he gave them from earliest childhood.

As a husband, he is perfect. Our love is blessed and we are made one by the Lord. He keeps us in perfect peace and our reunion will be filled with joy.

103

The ways that the children and I know him are precious, treasured thoughts but I also know what kind of American and military leader he is, for I have had the honor to share this part of his life with him. Gene is, without question, the most unselfish, honorable man I have ever known. He has deep compassion for people and is dedicated to making this nation what we all want it to be. He is loyal and would give his life for his country.

We believe that peace is still the beautiful word that was depicted in the Bible - not taking on the connotation that some revolutionists are trying to give it. We still get choked up when we see the American flag fluttering in the blue sky. We still feel that we must get right with God and then we can find the proper perspective to love our neighbor and live at peace with our brother.

Gene and the other dedicated men that are prisoners of war are waiting and wondering if we on the homefront are undergirding them with our support and our allegiance. Please continue to write. Urge our leaders to use the POWs as a bargaining power - release some of our men with each troop withdrawal. Some of our men have been there too long - six years. Those men have families who are sick with worry - they fear their loved one will never be able to make his adjustment back to society.

One more request - I grow more and more convinced that our answer lies in prayer. Pray for the return of all our men and, since the Lord does listen to us and answer our prayers, pray for our national and world leaders. Pray for love in the heart of this great nation and let it begin with us.

JEANNE WILBER
Columbia Cross Roads, RD 3

With the new year of 1971 came an even stronger resolution to continue the crusade for the POW's and MIA's and a fervent prayer that there would soon be closure to the prisoner issue and the war. I also prayed for strength to keep up the pace as requests for speaking increased and pressures mounted. I was thankful Mom could be with the children when I made quick day trips to Washington. The National League of

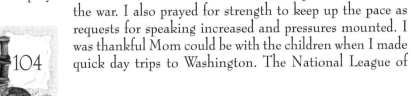

Families was planning a trip to Europe in May that I would be participating in.

In January I received a call from a woman in Scranton, PA who was in charge of World Day of Prayer that would be on March 4th. She told me there would be about seventy-five people attending. I agreed to do it and we decided to keep in touch, as the plans became more definite. I began praying about speaking to them, as I did before every presentation. First I had to confess all my sinful shortcomings and weaknesses and ask for His forgiveness in order for my heart to be in tune with Him. I was not a public speaker - only a wife, mother and homemaker who loved the Lord and wanted to serve Him. If I hadn't had this crusade for Gene and all the other men who were held captive or missing I would have never stepped up to a lectern.

The situation we wives were put in caused us to be in a position where the media was very much interested in us and we obliged because it was helping the message get out. I was most fortunate to have local news people that I could trust and feel comfortable with, but I could not wait for the time when Gene returned and I could melt back into private life. I really did not enjoy the notoriety but I became more comfortable with it because I did it to glorify God and I was always thankful that the media acknowledged my faith in Him. I truly wanted people to know that He loves us all the same. He provides each of us with the ability to choose exactly how much we want to serve Him. I fully realized that I had no reason to believe that God was showing favoritism to me for all the little and huge miracles that He worked out in my life every day - He does the same for anyone who completely trusts Him. I don't believe there is any reason for distinction in God's sight. Isn't it wonderful to know that we don't have to look around and say, "He loves her more" or "He loves him less." - We can joyfully say, "He loves me just as much as He loves anyone else - He loves us all the same!" Thank you God, for loving us equally - help us to love you more!

I always prayed ahead of time for the people I would be talking to - asking the Lord to fill me with the love that He had for them and that He would open their hearts and I would be able to convey the love He had available to each

105

one of them. It always made me nervous to think about being a "public speaker" so I chose to pretend that I was sitting at the kitchen table with them, having a conversation over a cup of tea or coffee. I was always aware that many of them had sufferings that were much worse than mine - I needed special help to fill their needs.

When I prayed about my prayer topic for the World Day of Prayer, I settled on Matthew 18:19 and when I talked to the chairperson two weeks later she said the theme of the program would be Matthew 18:19. We grew more excited each time we talked because we could see the Lord working out the plans through us and all the people she had praying about it. After they started to advertise - they had to change the location to a larger facility because over 500 had purchased luncheon tickets. As the time grew closer, 800 tickets were sold and the Mayor would be there to give me the key to the city. She told me a private plane from the Avoca airport would pick me up at the airport near Elmira on the morning of March 4th.

Two days before the luncheon, it started snowing here on the hill - it snowed and snowed! By Thursday morning, March 3rd, we could hardly see out some of our downstairs windows where the drifts were building up against the house. School was cancelled and the roads were plugged full so there was no traffic going by. I called the Elmira airport at 4:30 in the afternoon and they had closed the airport - there was a 19-foot drift in front of the hangar. I tried to call Mom to tell her but our line was dead. We had no way to communicate with the outside world. (Thank You Lord, that we still have electricity and our home is toasty warm!!) (Thank You, too, that the children are here with me! I love You!)

I kept praying through the night as I heard the wind roaring and whining but toward morning the wind stopped and the white stillness reflected through the windows. I knew the Lord wanted me to go to Scranton. His whole plan had pointed me in that direction - He would work this problem out.

106

I got up at my usual 5:30 AM and after devotions and breakfast I bathed and dressed in the clothes I had ready for the occasion. The children were eager to see how the whole thing would work out. I was thankful they were so dependable and would be able to take care of everything while I was gone. At 8:00 AM I took my post by a window in the family room so that I could see the snowdrifts where the road should be. It was very silent that morning and then in the distance we heard the sound of a road grader and then a snowmobile. Our friend Gordon was driving the grader and Gene's brother, Leslie, was on the snowmobile. They came in with a snowmobile suit that I put on over my dress. I put my purse, dress shoes and mink jacket in a bag, slipped on my snow boots, kissed the children good bye, and off I went to ride four miles on a snowmobile and another three miles - going three miles an hour on the grader. When we got to the main road, Pauline was waiting in her car and Mom was with her. We made it to Scranton on time. When we arrived there we learned that a bulldozer, snowplows and State Police to drive me to Scranton were trying to reach our home from the other direction.

The World Day of Prayer program was very meaningful and the people were wonderful. It was especially heart-warming for me because Reidun and also Bernie's parents were there. They lived near Wilkes Barre, which is only a few miles from Scranton. Bernie had gone to Kings College in that area and had been a star basketball player. Also Mr. and Mrs. Schweitzer had come for the occasion - they were the parents of the other officer that was televised with Gene on our anniversary. I was amazed and uplifted again at how God worked everything together for His good and how He was in our midst that day.

It was late in the day when we came to our road and found that it was still closed. We could see that attempts had been made to open it up but it was drifted full. I had to get home to the children and decided to walk the remaining 1-1/2 miles. It was a refreshing trudge and I did not mind the few struggles along the way because I would soon be home with my own family that I loved so very much! Precious Lord, thank You for the warmth of our love for each other!

107

From the beginning my plea had been for all of the prisoners and missing men; but after 1970 when I had the advantage of messages and the telecast, I felt that I was the fortunate one and I began to work and pray even more diligently for the other men. I was familiar with their personal stories because by now I was well acquainted with many of the wives. One of the reasons we enjoyed being with each other was that we could freely share our feelings, talk about questions we had about our husbands, compare effects the circumstances were having on our children and the fears of our own hearts: things that we couldn't share with our other friends because we worried that they would grow tired of our incessant need to talk about our men - it was one of the only ways we could keep the memory of them alive in our hearts. Most of us did not know each other's husbands but through our conversations, we began to feel that we knew them and as I prayed for each one, I grew to have great compassion and love for them. The ultimate goal was to see each family reunited and we often talked about that, saying, "I can't wait for you to meet my husband." But that was all small talk compared to our mission - the work we were doing for our husbands.

In May 1971, 165 of us from the National League of Families met in Washington. Our delegation left from Dulles Airport to fly to Geneva, Switzerland to attend several meetings of the International Committee of the Red Cross (ICRC) to appeal for support of the Geneva Convention. The international agreement was to be the subject of a May 24th meeting of international legal experts representing more than 30 countries among which would be the United States and the Soviet Union. Members of our group called on delegates to the ICRC meeting, to ask for their help in ensuring that all countries comply with the rules of the Geneva Convention which was signed by both parties to the conflict in Vietnam. We expressed our concern for the POW's and MIA's and we hoped that the countries represented would resolve to demand impartial inspection of the POW camps, a complete accounting of all prisoners and those missing, immediate release of the sick and wounded; and that mail flow would be in accordance with the provisions of the Geneva Convention.

They had not intended to discuss the POW issue but because of our presence it became a topic of concern by many ICRC members from countries other than the United States. The major general of the ICRC was most sympathetic.

Hanois fanger i dårlige kår

Krigsfangers hustruer ber om hjelp

De må leve i uvisshet om sine menns skjebne: Fra venstre fru Jean Wilber og fru Reidun Karlsen Rupinski

I left Geneva and the security of the delegation from the National League of Families to fly to Oslo, Norway where I had prearranged a meeting with Reidun, who by this time had left the States and moved back to her home

town in Larvik, Norway. We had an appointment with the Minister of Foreign Affairs and talked to him about our concerns for the POW's and MIA's. Norway was a member of NATO with us (the United States) and they also were on friendly terms with North Vietnam. They had an ambassador there. I had high hopes that they might be able to glean information about Bernie, using the leverage that he should be of particular interest to Norway because Reidun was one of their own citizens. We also talked to him about the issues the National League of Families had just presented to the ICRC. The Minister of Foreign Affairs was very sympathetic and gracious and was most sincere when he offered to help. After our meeting with him we were taken to a television studio where we were interviewed.

It was difficult to leave Reidun so quickly but I had to fly to Paris where I joined my group again. After a good night's rest we went to the building where the Peace Talks were in session. We were not allowed to enter the building where the conference was being held but the Gendarme gathered us together in a roped off area where we could watch delegation members as they walked in. The Paris press coverage of our presence was very favorable - they were impressed with our unity and solemnity. The newspaper articles said they appreciated our dignified attitude.

By the time I returned from Europe my dedication to find an answer for Reidun had escalated and then I received word from Norway that the efforts of their Ambassador had been fruitless. You can run all over the world seeking an answer but the more I prayed about it the more I realized that my only source of information was Gene - he knew the answer. As I worked in my garden that summer I prayed about the formulation of the letter - we were only allowed to mention the same immediate family names in our six-line form letter and I was having to pray that the addition of new names would not cause suspicion. In September I mailed it and prayed all the way to the mailbox - we had never had our letters connect in a way that we could respond to each other (some of our letters were nine months old when we got them). Besides, this was a bad year for mail - I hadn't heard from Gene since Christmas (nine months). I had put eleven or twelve names in one letter and in the very center of the list I

110

wrote "Reidun and Candy?" (Candy's husband was the other VF102 pilot who was missing.)

I stopped speaking but there was much to do at home. My tomato crop was huge so I had lots of canning to do and many other vegetables to harvest, freeze and can. In my spare time I continued to write letters - this is one I wrote to President Nixon:

September 14, 1971

His Excellency Richard M. Nixon
The President of the United States
The White House
Washington, DC

Dear President Nixon:

During these many months that you have been our President there have been times when I have wished that I could just walk up to your office, knock on the door, be granted permission to enter and talk to you. I realize the improbability of my wish. I also know what burdens you carry and I don't want to add to the tremendous weight.

My husband is a Prisoner of War in North Vietnam - perhaps you will recall that he was one of two prisoners interviewed on film at Christmas time. We consider ourselves fortunate to know that he is there - many of my friends know nothing after years of waiting. When I consider them and witness their despair, I find it hard to relate my personal feelings - but they do exist.

I have worked diligently to make the public aware of the plight of the Prisoners of War and Missing in Action. Two years ago I started speaking with great energy and wholehearted conviction. I felt I was doing what was best for Gene and I truly believed that once the American public was made aware of the situation, Hanoi would be swayed and our men would be released.

Now that summer is ending and my children are back in school it is time to start another round of campaigning but to tell the truth - I am tired! It hurts me to have to continually

111

defend Gene and our government when I am bombarded with questions about the war. All I know is that I am hopelessly in love with my husband and I want him home where he belongs. I remain loyal to my government and tearfully proud to be an American.

During the past Winter and Spring months it seemed that the Prisoner of War issue was brought before the public on frequent occasions. This gave me hope that positive action was being taken. I was growing excited with thoughts of our blissful reunion but now we hear nothing and my spirits are low.

Perhaps something is being done that I am not aware of - I cling to that satisfying thought. But there are moments of despair when I wonder if indeed he will even be home a year from now.

I realize that you must be considering all aspects of our involvement in Southeast Asia daily. You must get advice from thousands of Americans each day concerning this matter. In no way do I feel qualified to offer one small idea as to how to solve our problem. I trust you implicitly and you have my full support. I guess I just want you to know that my undaunted patience is suddenly being swept away by my leaping hungry heart. I want desperately for it to be over!

You must realize how I long to be reunited with Gene but I think I have an even greater desire. I want him to share the joy and pride as well as the moments of anticipation and deep concern of watching our four children change and develop. I want the children to know the priceless privilege of growing up under his wonderful guidance and direction. I want him to feel the love and respect they hold for him.

There has always been a special awesome expectancy about Christmas. We realize its full meaning here in our home and we are grateful for the Spirit of peace and joy that is renewed each year. The children have done well and I am proud of them but I don't want them to be without their Dad for one more Christmas season. I want us to be a complete family again!

Will you please help me!

Most sincerely,
Mrs. Walter E. Wilber

And one I wrote to the President of North Vietnam follows:

3 Dec. 1971

Dear Mr. President,

You may think it very presumptuous of me to write directly to you but I feel you are the only person in the world that has the power to honor my request.

My husband, Walter Eugene Wilber 539459, is being held somewhere in your country. He was shot down and captured near Vinh on 16 June 1968.

My humble request is that you please release him. My reasons are not calculated - I have no elaborate argument, I simply love him. He is my life. I want to care for him and comfort him. I want him home so our four children can know the priceless privilege of growing under his guidance and direction.

Knowing him as I do I can assure you that he has proven himself to be an honorable man, in every respect, during his internment in your land. I would ask you to check with his prison commander to learn if this is not true. He is gentle, kind, trustworthy, considerate and conscientious. I know these attributes have not changed.

Christmas is the season of Peace, Love and Joy. It is also the season of giving. My fervent prayer is that the Nations involved in the conflict in Southeast Asia will find the desire to give - by lowering the barricades of animosity, softening their attitude toward one another and finding a mutual ground for understanding and agreement. If each strives to work toward the Brotherhood of all mankind we can achieve 'Peace on Earth, Good will toward Men!'

I realize how much you have on your mind and how many demands are made upon you, but I pray you will find it in your heart to answer my request. I will never cease being grateful to you!

May the blessings of Christmas be yours and may the people of your nation find much happiness in the coming year.

Most sincerely,

113

One day when I was doing my weekly cleaning upstairs I noticed a picture of a Christmas tree on Mark's desk. It was so neatly done that I had to pick it up to admire it and I noticed that there were a few sheets of notebook paper beneath it. The one on top had a decorated tree with presents under it and a boy looking at the tree. In the upper corner was a manger scene with Mary, Joseph, Baby Jesus, a lamb and a star was shining brightly above. I lifted the picture and all he had written on the next page was:

"Dear President Nixon"

The next page said:

"Dear Mr. Press,

My Mom _____ "

(Mr. Press was his beloved teacher.)

The next page said

"Dear Mr. Press"

What a struggle he was having. All of these pages had been done neatly in red ink with a firm hand but the feelings that were in his heart couldn't come out in words.

Then I looked at the next page. This sentence was written, very weakly, in pencil with no salutation:

"You don't no how much I miss my Dad this Christmas."

When a mother sees her children hurt she weeps. Thank you God, that another year is almost over.

THE PATCHWORK of MY LIFE

Chapter 16

The Conflict Within

There comes a time when we have to face an underlying problem. One of the reasons I stopped speaking in 1971 was that Gene was meeting with every anti-war contingent that went to North Vietnam and nearly all of them called or came here to tell me about it. Ramsey Clark (the former U.S. Attorney General) called and talked a long time. Our conversation was pleasant and informative and I appreciated the fact that he did not try to change my life or convert me - he only called to tell me how Gene looked and about his general condition. When Jane Fonda returned from visiting him, she had her secretary call me so it was not very helpful, but Miss Fonda's presence there met with such negative publicity here that I wanted to crawl in a hole. Two gentlemen, Mr. Livingston and Mr. Caldwell, came here to our home and were very kind - no pressure just further news about Gene. Then on February 25, 1972, Dr. George Wald, the Nobel Prize winner from Harvard University called and talked until I was drained. It was a very difficult day filled with confusion and tension. He was very adamant about my getting actively involved in the anti-war organization - I should be taking the "kids" to meetings and join the anti-war group. I was letting Gene down - he wasn't concerned about getting out. When I talked about my prayers for Gene he said, "Your prayers, hopes and faith are not enough or what Gene wants but if that little ritual pleases you, then do it."

For two hours after he hung up I could hardly move. My little world was on a rug that had been pulled out from under me. My heart ached. Gene had been gone for nearly four years. I could not let anyone sever our oneness. My devotion to Gene was rock hard —thanks to God! My loyalty to my

country was stronger than ever. I had to get myself back together before our precious children came home from school.

Remember how hectic our lives were before Gene left for Vietnam? There were so few minutes with him that I always had to grab every one that I could. One day when he came home from work and the children had finished their delightful arousing greeting, I followed him to our bedroom. While he removed his uniform blouse, hung it up and put his cap away I stood on the foot of the bed to talk to him. From the time we were first married I couldn't get big enough to tell him how much I loved him or something really important - unless I climbed up on a kitchen chair or a stool or two steps up the stairs or on a stepladder and then - when I hugged him I could rest his head on me and hold him close while I let him know what was on my mind. In our bedroom that afternoon I had my arms around his neck and he looked up at me to see what I had on my mind. My question was serious, "How can you, as a Christian, kill people?" He was serious, too and told me that they did not fly over populated areas to bomb. They were after roads, bridges, trucks - anything that had to do with transportation. We had been fortunate to spend all those years between Korea and Vietnam just keeping the peace in foreign waters.

Now as I recalled the scene I thought also about my daily prayers that his captors would have compassion for him and knowing Gene's sincere interest in people I couldn't imagine him being belligerent over there. I also began to realize that "peace" was a good word when he left and the Paris Peace Talks were in the planning stage and we hoped together that there would be a speedy negotiated settlement. I knew how loyal Gene was to his service.

Accusations were made that Gene did these things in order for him to get better treatment and that would be impossible to believe. Gene always let people go before him and took a place near the end of the line, he would never eat steak and let our children eat hot dogs, every one else at a table had to be served first - I could go on and on; I know his nature and he will **never** change! I began to think that he had come to the conclusion that the only way all the prisoners would get home would be for the war to end and that is all he was asking for.

I was left with one question, "Why would Gene break the Code of Conduct and speak out?" Certainly not for personal gain - I knew that for a fact! And what personal gain comes from breaking ranks with your comrades - it takes courage to stand for your convictions and for what you believe to be truth. Then why? Did he share the desperation that one prisoner wrote to his wife, "Must I die here?" Even Gene, on Susan's tenth birthday, wrote, "I pray I can see you before another ten years go by." Was he using this as an opportunity and a means to be truly doing his part to end the war and free the prisoners? That is what I was doing - I was driven to do my small part. In effect our government, the National League of Families and the Paris Peace Talks were trying to do the same thing - bring an end to the war and set the prisoners free.

After my conversation with Dr. Wald, I revised my speech and this is what I added:

> *"After all this time I still seek the key to the release of our prisoners and a complete accounting of our missing in action. I can see the various sides and I can hear how right each side feels that they are. When I weigh the arguments of everyone it leads to further frustration and the knowledge that after all these months and years I still can't see the end.*
>
> *One thing I have watched develop has been the anti-war element. I must admit that I have been turned off by them because I have disapproved of their demonstrations. The revolutionists and radicals have shouted "peace" while desecrating our flag, they have caused unrest among our young people and they have been undermining the very structure of our great nation. It has been my observation also that with their attempts to end the war they have indeed prolonged it. Because of their questionable political leanings many loyal Americans have feared being linked with them if they admitted that they wanted an end to the war and peace. Consequently the voices that would be heard and respected have been silenced for too long.*

118

I am well aware that Gene and all the other prisoners of war will not come home until our involvement ends. Naturally this is a serious matter to me because Gene is my very life.

Is there a way we can say we want the war to end without being labeled "Anti-war?" Can't there be a better title - like "Loyal American Peacemakers" or "Patriots for Peace?" But why must we be categorized if we just say what is in our heart? I think it is time for the silent majority to speak!

We are members of a great nation. I am so proud to be an American that my eyes fill up with tears sometimes when I think about it. Perhaps my awareness of the moments I would like to capture and retain for Gene has strengthened my appreciation for the beauty of the land, the warmth of our people, the richness of our heritage and the real privilege it is to live in these United States.

Maybe this devotion explains why my concern extends beyond the prisoner issue. It disturbs me to see the inner conflict the war has caused here at home and my heart goes out to our young men who go to fight and give their lives for a cause that some of them question. Instead of a heroes welcome many are despised when they return.

My only suggestions are to urge you and have you urge others to offer your supportive, constructive opinions to members of our government and anyone in authority who can help the situation. It is great to live in a democracy where our voices can be heard. Just remember that it is our job to strengthen and undergird the people that we have elected. They want to know our feelings so they can serve us more completely."

119

Chapter 17

Another Miracle

In March 1972 I received a letter from Gene and praise be to God!, it was his reply to my September 1971 letter. He wrote "Dearest Jeanne, I can only send my deepest sympathy to Reidun and Candy ——." I knew then that Bernie and Chuck must have gone down with their planes. I called the Bureau of Naval Personnel in Washington, D.C., and read the letter to the officer in charge of P.O.W. Matters. He knew us and said he wished it could be possible for me to go to Norway to see and inform Reidun - he knew I loved her and would comfort her. He also realized that Reidun was uncomfortable with casualty assistance officers. Oh! How I wished I could go to be with her but I told him it was out of the question at that time. I did not explain to him that my trip to Europe and the flights to Washington kept my budget fairly tight. I always planned ahead and saved for the trips but I didn't have enough surplus right then. I received an allotment from Gene's pay each month to run the household and the remainder of his pay went into a savings for him and though I could have withdrawn from his account, I tried not to touch it.

As soon as I put the phone back in its cradle the phone rang and it was our old dear friend, Clyde. He was by this time a Commander in the Coast Guard, stationed in Washington, DC and he piloted the Commandant of the Coast Guard's plane (a Gulfstream II). He called to tell me that the Commandant was in Mexico and Clyde would be flying back down there to get him but after their return they would be leaving the following Monday for London, Copenhagen and Oslo. He knew my friend Reidun lived near there and he wondered if he could do anything for me - call on her? Take her out for dinner? I could hardly believe my ears and I was saying to myself, "Thank You

Lord, thank You!" I expressed my joy in hearing from him and explained that I had Reidun on my heart right then but I could not talk about it because it was classified information. I told him I would send a birthday present for Michelle that he could deliver. I wanted to say more but I couldn't. We visited briefly and then hung up. I was hoping the Lord was working out another miracle and I had that tingle of excitement but I tried to put it out of my mind. How could I even think that they would allow me on that flight? Even if I was asked, I couldn't go - I had eleven speeches the following week - three on the day they were leaving and I had to honor those obligations. I checked my calendar and thought why couldn't it be week after next? There were no commitments and that was unusual.

Within 30 minutes Clyde called back and said he had talked to the Commandant and he wanted me to be his guest on the flight. I tried to suppress my joy and I told him how very much I appreciated their thoughtfulness but I had obligations that I had to meet. He then said, "Oh, I forgot to tell you - the trip has been changed to ———," and the dates he gave me were the exact dates I had free on my calendar.

Oh, Precious Lord Jesus, how can You be so good to me? How can I ever repay You? I will honor You forever and give all the glory to You as long as I live! Thank You! I know You are always in control but thank You for these glimpses we get of Your loving care!

The Special Assistant for P.O.W. Matters was glad to hear that I could go to Norway and when I called Reidun she was delighted to learn that I had an opportunity to go and spend a few days with her. There was one minor discomfort that I had to contend with. A few days before I received the letter from Gene, that set this whole chain of events in motion, I had fallen the full length of our stairs and had fractured a vertebra in my back. I was immobile for two or three days but I forced myself back in motion to keep up with all I had to do. Even when I went on the trip the gnawing pain kept me uncomfortable but I took an inflated ring to sit on which helped to some degree. The only time I was in real agony was when I had to carry my luggage (we didn't have the helpful little rollers that are provided on luggage now) or get in and out of a car.

Clyde's twin brother, Lee, (who had been a member of our wedding party, lived near Elmira and was the chief pilot for Corning Glass, Inc) called me the day after Clyde and I had talked. Lee offered to fly me to Washington and escort me to the Coast Guard hangar to meet Clyde. I was very grateful for those dear friends!

It was good to be with Reidun again and after Michelle went to sleep the night I arrived I let Reidun read Gene's letter. We talked for many hours and though neither of us knew the circumstances of Bernie's death - Gene's words confirmed it for her. It really came as no surprise to Reidun but still it was difficult to get the news. At least now she could put closure on that part of her life and continue on. We were both glad I had five more days to be with them.

Chapter 18

Explo 72

The heat was overwhelming when I stepped off the plane in Dallas, Texas, that early June day in 1972. "Why did I wear a suit?" I thought to myself, and why hadn't I remembered how hot it would be when I was making my preparations in the coolness of our Pennsylvania hills. It wasn't as if I had never been in Texas - we had lived there for 3-1/2 years! Within minutes the woman I was to stay with found me and welcomed me with such genuine, friendly Texas hospitality that I forgot the oppressive heat and though we had never seen each other before, we were immediate friends - that is what Jesus can do to a relationship.

We picked up my luggage, put it in the trunk of her car and went to her home where I met her husband and children - what a nice family! "Thank you, Lord, for a safe place to stay while I'm away from my children - keep them in your loving arms until I return, and ever after also."

Quite a few months earlier, Gary Taylor, a representative of Campus Crusade for Christ, had called from California to ask me to lead a seminar on Prayer for the Prisoners of War, at Explo '72, in Dallas. Campus Crusade for Christ was sponsoring the event to be held on June 12 in the Cotton Bowl. It turned out to be the largest revival meeting for youth in the history of the United States up to that time, with 100,000 in attendance, of which 80,000 were young people. The six-day evangelical conference consisted of training seminars, prayer meetings, a music festival and rallies at the Cotton Bowl. Billy Graham was there to speak, was named honorary chairman and attended many of the events. Bill Bright, leader of Campus Crusade for Christ International, was in charge and had invited many athletes and

celebrities to the event. I particularly appreciated talking with Jim Erwin, a Christian astronaut, who had a real interest in learning more about the POWs. Some people expected Explo to be a super organized rock festival, but instead it was an expression of the spiritual yearnings of American youth. The adult community in Dallas found Explo '72 to be a peaceful alternative to the protest movements. My hostess and I had slow drives from her home to the Conference Center due to the heavy traffic, and especially the big night at the Cotton Bowl. As we inched along or waited bumper-to-bumper, we had beautiful experiences conversing from car to car or reaching out to clasp the hand of a young person in the car beside us. My heart was refreshed to see the love of Christ wash over everyone there and I kept wishing I had my big boys with me.

My remarks for the seminar that I led follow:

> *I am deeply moved to be here today. Surely something wonderful is going to happen as a result of this explosive week.*

> *The Bible verse I want to use is Matthew 18:19 - I will quote it from the Phillips translation: "And I tell you once more that if two of you on earth agree in asking for anything it will be granted to you by my Heavenly Father." These are the words of Jesus and I believe them. He also said, "For whenever two or three people come together in my name I am there right among them!"*

> *How wonderful to know that He is here "right among us." My prayer now is that each heart will be open to Him. Let Him touch you. Be filled with His love, joy, peace, patience, gentleness, goodness and faith. He gives these blessings freely if we but love Him. Isn't He wonderful!*

> *With Him in our midst we feel a bond of affection and understanding.*

> *When Gary Taylor called and asked me to talk to you he expressed the need for prayer for the wives*

125

*of Prisoners of War and Missing In Action. My im-
mediate reaction was probably much like that of any
P.O.W. wife. "We need prayer for our men - if we can
reach 100,000 people let's pray for the release of all
our Prisoners of War and a complete accounting of
our Missing in Action. - We have a miracle for God to
perform so why not get right down to business."*

*After thinking this over Gary's idea makes sense
- I have come back down to earth and can look at this
with new perspective. Perhaps we have been forget-
ting the required groundwork because our hearts have
been focused on the ultimate goal. We wives have been
in firm agreement about the goal but when Jesus said,
"If we agree in asking it will be granted" could He
have meant -not only agreeing on the worthiness of
the petition but also agreeing that He is omnipotent
and we must put our faith and trust in Him? It seems
only fitting that if we are to expect a miracle from
Him we should love and serve Him first.*

*I realize that in my own life things have to be
right - my wavelength with the Lord has to be clean,
clear and crisp. He hears me best when I am in tune
with Him. When I carry frustrations and burdens in
my heart and forget to confess my shortcomings and
ask His forgiveness my prayers seem shallow and
unfulfilled because of my lack of sincerity - but when I
remember - like a fresh ray of sunlight - that He loves
me and really wants to lift these burdens from me I
am uplifted. Cleansed by Him I feel His presence
and I am filled with joy because I expect a miracle
and I feel the exhilaration of knowing my prayer is
heard and answered. It is at these times of unclutter
that the proper attitude for real prayer comes.*

*Knowing this in relation to my own experience I
can understand that we wives do need prayer. If we
don't have a personal relationship with Jesus we need
it! The more we can unite in Him the more powerful*

our basic agreement will be to obtain our ultimate goal. Let us get right with God and trust in Him to bring our men home!

You know - it really seems good to be with military wives again. Two years ago the children and I moved from Virginia Beach to a remote area in Northern PA. So I have been away from the way of life that I had known for nearly 18 years. You must realize the closeness I feel toward you and also to those of you who are not military just because we are sisters in Him. I want to ask all of you now to enter the awareness that lives with the P.O.W. - M.I.A families every moment - waking or sleeping.

Our men are strong, brave and gallant but they are also sweet, real and in need of some tender loving care. We want more than anything to give this to them.

Paul said in his letter to the Galations: "Bear ye one another's burdens and so fulfill the law of Christ." Will you bear this burden with us? In this way we will all be in agreement when we pray. We will be united in our crusade.

Now for that ultimate goal. It seems that over the last three years we have scratched every earthly surface searching for our ray of hope. For the five years prior to that our government was making vain attempts in private negotiation. Our men can't wait much longer. For those who have been there six, seven or eight years - yesterday was too late.

So often we make vain attempts to accomplish the impossible by ourselves but all things are possible through Him. Why do we frantically run down each blind alley seeking our answer when His way is there - spread out clearly before us?

127

He can melt hearts of stone and fill them with compassion. He can break all barriers and set the prisoner free. Our loving God can accomplish this. All we need is faith to believe. His powers are released when we go to Him in prayer.

Let us pray for the release of every man held captive and an accounting for the missing every moment it burdens our heart. Let us visualize that wonderful march to freedom as we pray and we will experience what I call the joy of faith. Believe it and it shall be done!

Because of your concern you will share in the joy of seeing those men come back to this nation they love so well - to bask in Freedom's Holy Light and live where man still cares for his fellow man.

I have my own vision of that homecoming. I know that glorious day will come. I can almost taste the relief of running into Gene's arms with four eager children in our midst. The Lord will be smiling on us that day and a family of six - a whole - complete family of six - will bow down together and pour out praises of thanksgiving to Him!

Will you pray without ceasing? I beg you - please do this for them!

128

129

Chapter 19

The Final Countdown

One of my concerns when Gene started broadcasting and being interviewed was how it would be accepted within military circles. I was grateful that the POW MIA wives treated me the same and our Navy friends remained true to us. On several occasions in Washington I was made thankful when officials spoke to me and expressed their respect for Gene; and I almost sensed an air of protection toward me. At a dinner meeting I was sitting at a round table of eight wives and Secretary of Defense, Melvin Laird came down from the speakers table, leaned over me and asked how I was doing - he was very gracious and I was honored by his genuine concern. At another dinner I was again at a table with other

Between Secretary of the Navy, John Warner
and Admiral Zumwalt

wives and an aid for Admiral Zumwalt came to me and said the Admiral wanted me to sit with him at the speakers table. When I went up, they placed me between Admiral Zumwalt, Chief of Naval Operations, and Secretary of the Navy John Warner. That summer of 1972 I received a letter telling me that Gene had been promoted to Captain. To me, these were all good indicators that everything was all right.

Trying to figure out how to let Gene know about his promotion was fun. When you can only fill in a six-line form once each month and you are limited to write about family and health, it is hard not to be repetitive in your letters. So I welcomed the opportunity to try to hide this good news in my letter. When a Navy officer makes the rank of Captain more gold is added to his uniform and they call the gold design on the visor of the cap "scrambled eggs". Fortunately I received the news during the summer, so I itemized vegetables we were eating from the garden, and added, "We are enjoying more scrambled eggs", and he knew we didn't have any chickens. Gene got the message and knew exactly what I meant.

Besides the one letter each month, we could send an extra card and package at Christmas. We could also send letters through the Committee of Liaison and with groups traveling to Hanoi, so all in all I probably sent about 75 letters to Gene.

Autumn of 1972 was like an emotional roller coaster ride. In October huge headlines appeared saying "Peace is Eminent" or "Peace is at Hand." Our hopes escalated and we were excited - the children and I even did a little dancing around the house and waited eagerly for additional news. Our phone rang frequently and there was a happy air of anticipation throughout our home. But then our high hopes were dashed to the ground when nothing happened and the bombing was resumed. It was difficult to get through the Christmas season that year.

By early January we felt more hopeful and yet we did not dare claim the feeling. We knew the damage that disappointment could do to our already frayed emotions. We just kept praying and listening to every newscast.

Waiting - 1973

Our reaction was strangely subdued and tranquil when we heard the news on Saturday, January 27, 1973 that the conflict was over, there had finally been a settlement and peace had been signed. The prisoners would be freed. Bruce and Tom were both at work but Mark and Susan were home with me and we were extremely grateful but at the same time cautious. For nearly five years we had been waiting and now the waiting would be over. The unbelievable was coming true and yet we were so calm and reserved. Perhaps the Lord was shedding an added sprinkling of patience over us to help us through the last few weeks of waiting. Besides, "It's not over until it's over" and for me - it would not be over until I was in Gene's arms again!

For years I had been trying to write the letter to Gene that would be kept in a Navy file to be given to him when he was released but my attempts were futile. I just could not project my mind into the joy of the moment. Now I had to write it and this was my last letter to Gene:

My Most Precious Gene,

It is early Sunday morning - 28 Jan. 1973. It seems that I woke up with a lighter heart. We are at peace, our involvement is over and best of all - you will be free at last. My reserved emotions haven't let me realize these things with full impact. I feel strangely relieved and tearfully thankful.

We have much to catch up on and we will have our lifetime to do it. I just want you to know that my love for you has been magnified and grown with each passing day. If ever it was tested - it has been with this long separation and I am so grateful to the Lord that you have always stayed so fresh in my heart and mind. He has kept us one - so joyfully. Little thoughts of you have brought happiness to each day and my desire to be deserving of you has been an easy task because you are such a wonderful one to love.

I am delighted to say - Welcome Home - and hurry honey! The children and I will meet you and will be full of love and kisses. Oh - my dearest Gene - I do love you and most sincerely honey - you are my very life.

Your ever loving wife

Jeanne

The days following the peace agreement made me feel as if I was caught in a whirlwind. I wanted the house to be extra clean for Gene's homecoming so I scurried around doing my cleaning between phone calls, interviews and the general excitement of family and friends and watching the news to keep track of the release. Within days we learned that the men would be airlifted from Hanoi to Clark Air Force Base in the Philippines in three groups and Gene would be on the first plane carrying 143 prisoners of war to freedom on Feb. 12, 1973. I watched with Bruce and Tom through the night and woke Mark and Susan before the plane landed. We watched at 3:30 AM when Gene disembarked from the aircraft and I was thrilled to

Capt. Wilber saluting the American flag upon his arrival at Clark Air Base in the Philippines following his release from North Vietnam.

see his snappy salute, smiling face and easy stride as he walked with his natural military bearing. The reality was beginning to hit us as, with watery eyes, we gave each other joyful hugs.

There was little time left for sleep that night, but the children went to bed and a restful peace came over our household. Grateful satisfaction washed over us. Cobwebby, numbed emotions began to come alive again and as the remnants of the burden were being lifted, God in all His glory helped us celebrate. He gave us the most spectacular dawn I have ever seen!

Morning sometimes awakens sleepily yawning, rubbing its eyes and gradually coming to life, but this one made a bounding entrance. Generally the sunlight comes through the curtained windows on tiptoe, but not so for this grand occasion! Bright sunshine streamed in - as if to shout, "Ta da - I'm here!!" How could anyone keep from smiling at all that enthusiasm? I hurried to the window to see what was happening. Everything on our hill was aglow! A fresh covering of clean snow would have been enough but God poured a thin coating of ice over every single surface - a delicate glazing to catch the sunlight and cause its reflections to dance. The sight was so breathtakingly beautiful that I had to step outside to get a closer look and make sure I saw every detail in order to keep the picture in my mind's eye forever.

134

The air smelled so pure that it had a cleansing effect to my whole spirit. I felt a reverence - like I had stepped into a glorious cathedral. The rising sun spread its soft and beautiful fan that morning with its opalescent rays reaching upward toward heaven through the bluest of skies and cascaded down again through the ice crystals that seemed to hang still in the air. The trees and shrubs shimmered and sparkled like diamonds - every branch, limb and twig was encased in ice. God even provided music - not with angelic voices singing "Gloria" in twelve-part harmony from heaven above or the magnificent, deep resonance of a pipe organ echoing from the distant hill. As I stood there in thankful adoration, I could hear delicate music and realized that a gentle whisper of air was causing the tree tops to move. The ice that surrounded each twig made it a tiny wind chime - could it be the very breath of God?

The streams of light that shone through the trees refracted and tiny rainbows danced in the branches while other beams hit the more rigid surfaces of the lawn and driveway, sending shafts of light up to the sky again. My cup was running over as I shook myself from this spellbound state - I had to wake the children to let them savor this unbelievable morning, this gift from God, with me. Again I was filled with the thought, "It is I who should be doing something sacrificial for You for all You have done for us, and yet You in all your mercy and love keep giving and giving and giving to us. But I know, all you want is my heart. I give it again to You."

The display lasted for many hours and while we enjoyed it we were learning that all of the people in the valleys around us were unaware of the beauty we beheld. As relatives and friends came to be with us that day, they were as jubilant and stirred within as we were because the show of lights and dancing ice were only on our hilltop.

The following newspaper article tells about our first phone call:

135

Hanging Up Is Difficult

The difficult part of a 15-minute phone conversation between Navy Capt. and Mrs. W. Eugene Wilber was hanging up. Finally, Capt. Wilber did it.

"I just couldn't hang up that telephone! He kept saying, 'Okay, hang up now, honey,' and I couldn't do it. I told him to, and he couldn't either," said Mrs. Jeanne Wilber of Coryland, near Columbia Cross Roads, after receiving the long-awaited call from her husband at 5:50 this morning.

Mrs. Wilber had waited up all through the previous night to see her husband on television as he and 142 other prisoners of war landed at Clark Air Force Base in the Philippines.

After that, she was expecting the telephone call at any minute. But it didn't come.

136

"By 11 last night, I was drooping. So I went to bed - but I took the telephone to bed with me. I put it on his side of the bed," said the laughing, happy Mrs. Wilber.

Mrs. Wilber had had numerous false alarms through the day, as the news media and friends checked to see if she had heard from her husband.

'I was afraid maybe he hadn't been able to get through because the line was busy. But he said he hadn't been able to call earlier because so many men had to make calls. And then, he didn't want to call in the night,' Mrs. Wilber said.

He also wanted to call when the children were home, but one child was missing when the call came through. Mark, 12, Susan, 10 and Tom, 17, talked with their father, but Bruce, 19, had already left for work.

Mrs. Wilber said that her husband sounded *'just wonderful.'*

'I didn't cry, we were both just laughing and bubbling over. I can't even express it, we were so happy. He told me he checked out fine but there were just a few problems and he'd have to be in a hospital in this country for a little while,' Mrs. Wilber said.

'I told him I'd be the only medicine he'd need. He liked that.'

Mrs. Wilber expects to see her husband within a week but she isn't sure when yet. She will be notified by her casualty officer and she and her children will be at a hospital at an undisclosed location to greet him.

'I think they'll keep them in California for a day to rest because it's such a long trip,' Mrs. Wilber said.

Then the Wilbers can begin planning their lives together, after a five-year separation.

'He asked me if I wanted him to retire and I told him that whatever he wanted would be all right with me but I didn't want him to make any hasty decisions. We'll talk about it later,' Mrs. Wilber said.

137

'We just want to be here together and live a happy normal life. We both said we never want to be separated again.'

(You see - he **does** go to the end of the line!)

The men were taken to the base hospital where over 60 doctors examined the freed prisoners and for the most part the men were healthy. The doctors had planned a bland diet to nurse their digestive systems but most of the men wanted American food so they got it. Gene had a steak dinner and a milkshake for his first meal. On Valentine's Day he sent me red roses! Could life really be on its way to getting back to normal?

139

Chapter 20

A Joyous Reunion

The day finally arrived for us to meet at the Philadelphia Naval Hospital. Our Casualty Assistance Officer, Gene's parents, the children and I flew from Elmira to Philadelphia. We checked in at a motel near the hospital and then in the late evening went to the hospital. We were interviewed by the news media who had their lights, cameras and microphones set up in the hospital lobby. Then we were escorted to the 12th floor. The entire floor was empty and the floors of the long halls shone brightly with wax. We were taken to a window rimmed solarium filled with exotic plants and flowers where Mother and Dad would wait until the children and I could greet him and then they would be able to join us. The children and I were then led down the wide hall to Gene's suite. We went in the living room which was nicely furnished and had large windows that overlooked the long boulevard drive that made its way to the entrance of the hospital, curved and then went its long distance back to the busy street. From our high lookout we would have a birds eye view of Gene when they arrived. We checked out the suite - beyond the large living room was a white tile bathroom that opened to the bedroom on the other side. It was very comfortable and I was sure Gene would appreciate it - especially in comparison with the cell he had lived in for so long.

We were forewarned by a corpsman that Gene was on his way. From the window where Bruce, Tom, Mark, Susan and I stood we saw the motorcade leave the highway and turn onto the boulevard that led to the hospital. The entourage was made up of all black cars and the center one was a limousine. When they came to a stop at the entrance, uniformed men hurriedly went to stand at attention and open the door of the limousine. Gene stepped out of the opened door and when he stood

(the children and I were all laughing and saying, "There he is") he returned the salute of the other men and was briskly led to the entrance. We knew he would be detained in the lobby by the news people but it wasn't long until we heard the elevator doors at the end of the hall and then we could hear the resounding echo of their footsteps as they came quickly down the empty hallway.

The children and I stood in a row in the center of the room and when they came into our view from the doorway it was as if a light shone around him and when he saw us he gasped and his knees buckled for a brief second. The next moment we were in each other's arms! What a joyous reunion as he studied each face and each child's height and we could not keep our eyes off him - he was so *real*! After a few minutes Gene's parents were brought in and that was a happy reunion also.

It had been midnight when Gene arrived at the hospital. After we all visited for about 30 minutes, our CACO took Mother, Dad and the children to the motel so Gene and I could be alone for a little longer and then the CACO would take me to the motel. Gene and I sat on the sofa and started talking - we had so much to tell each other that the room was never quiet. His warm sincere eyes and ready smile were such a welcome sight to me. I looked at my watch and it was 6:00 AM - where had the night gone? Our poor CACO - we hurried down the hall and he sleepily came to attention. Gene and I were so happy to be together again. How good it was to hug and kiss him goodbye knowing it would only be for a short time - we would all be back for Sunday dinner.

I quietly entered our room so I would not wake the children. It was 6:30 when I got in bed and Tom came over, knelt beside me and asked how Dad really was. I assured him that Dad was fine - Tom hugged me and went back to bed. Thank you Lord, for all my blessings!

I awoke feeling rested, refreshed and excited - what a happy day - we would be seeing Gene in a short time! Thank You Lord, for this glorious day! We will surely rejoice! I slipped out of bed so I would not wake Susan; Tom and Mark were sound asleep in the other bed and Bruce was sleeping in the adjoining room. I stepped over to the window where a sliver of sun-light was coming through an opening in the drapes. My watch said 7:10 - I shook it - it must have stopped. I went to the bedside table and took the travel alarm clock to the sliver of light - it read 7:10! I had soundly slept for only 35 minutes and was as refreshed as I would have been with eight hours sleep. Oh -what a beautiful day! Life is great - Gene is for real! God has truly taken good care of us!

I soon had everyone up and called Mother and Dad's room so we could set a time to go for breakfast. We all had so much to talk about that we lingered over breakfast and then we went back to our rooms to pack. In the evening Mother, Dad and our CACO were going to fly home with the children in order for them to go to school and work the following day. Mom would be waiting at home for the children and I would be staying on to be in the hospital each day with Gene.

The morning went by quickly and at noon cars arrived to take us to the hospital. We could hardly wait to see Gene again. He looked clean and refreshed and was in very good spirits. A beauti-ful table had been set up in the middle of the living room. It was meticulously set with white linen tablecloth and napkins, massive silverware, official looking chinaware, flowers and a large fruit bowl. At dinnertime we were seated and served a delicious meal. The conversation was relaxed and pleasant. Gene had many stories about his meals of bread and watery cabbage soup with no salt or meat to season it - only cabbage and lots of water. Naturally he savored the food that was set before him and, as he had done before he went to Vietnam, he wanted everyone to "clean up their plate" but he seemed even more aware of waste now.

After dinner we moved to the chairs and sofa in order that the steward could clear the table and put it back in its place against the wall. It was then arranged with a runner, the flowers, a bowl of fresh fruit and plates of chocolates, nuts and mints. Gene and his Dad were visiting on the sofa and Bruce and I were standing in the middle of the room talking to each other. Bruce started to eat a chocolate and when he bit into it half of it broke off and fell to the floor. He bent over to pick it up and started to go toward the wastebasket in the bathroom to dispose of

it. Gene stopped conversing with his Dad and asked Bruce what he was going to do with the candy. Bruce said, "Throw it away," and Gene said, "Bring it to me - I'll eat it." We all laughed and Gene laughed with us but we sadly realized how little he had in prison and how precious even a morsel was to him.

For some strange reason Gene contested the official plan that he would remain in the hospital each night while I went to the motel. Even though we would spend our days and eat all meals together, he didn't seem very satisfied. As evening came and our family members had departed, Gene excused himself and went down the hall to talk to an officer in charge. He came back smiling and said, "Let's go." A driver escorted us to a waiting car and took us to the motel saying he would return for us at 7:00 AM. Gene never used the hospital bed again and I was glad.

The days became routine as Gene underwent medical and psychological testing from after breakfast to lunchtime and each afternoon until 4:00 or 4:30. It was neat having the whole 12th floor to our selves - I could read or write in our room or in the solarium and sometimes he took me to meet and talk with his doctors. A few times the driver took me to downtown Philadelphia to shop for clothes for Gene - he had left Hanoi in Vietnamese clothes and then the Navy had supplied him with a uniform in the Philippines so there were quite a few things he needed. Every evening our driver took us to a lovely restaurant, waited while we dined and then returned us to the motel.

On Friday, Feb. 23rd, Gene was able to go home for the first time. We flew into the Elmira Airport and were greeted by 3000 people. Gene was truly moved by their welcome. The Boy Scouts put out a red carpet and Gene saluted them when he emerged from the plane. Our children were the first ones we greeted and then Gene's sister, Beverly, and his two brothers, Leslie and Richard, were in line for their long awaited hug from their brother. We were led to a platform where many officials were waiting - our friend, Lee was Master of Ceremonies. It was a warm and wonderful welcome and Gene was glad to be back. He told them he appreciated the way they had taken care of the children and me while he was gone.

143

(Thank You God - it is over!)

144

HOMECOMING–Navy Capt. W. Eugene Wilber of Columbia Cross Roads is happy to come home in 1973 after being in a prisoner of war camp. His son, Mark, shows he's glad his father's back.

Tom drove us home and people waved at us along the way. Our small town of Daggett had a large banner suspended high above the road. When we came to our Hickory Road, Gene grew more excited and when we reached the edge of our land and went over the crest of the hill he could see our home 1/4 mile away. It was great to be home again!

We traveled back and forth to Philadelphia spending the weekdays at the hospital and the weekends at home. Every weekend Mom presented us with one and sometimes two laundry baskets full of mail and we began to realize that we would never be able to answer it all but we knew also that our love for the American people was reinforced.

Gene wanted a vacation with the children. He realized that Bruce at 19 would not be able to go on trips with us much longer. When we talked about our plans, Gene kept going back to the same thought - he wanted to see Reidun and be able to talk to her about the accident. In April all six of us went to Europe and we are very thankful we did - it was memorable for all of us.

We planned to go to church on Easter Sunday in London and arrived there on Saturday. We checked in at a lovely hotel. We had tried to get adjoining rooms but were unable to. Mark and Tom were close by but Bruce and Susan were one floor down. We had specific rules for the trip: Bruce was responsible for Susan, Tom would take care of Mark; all six of us would stay together at all times. Gene's and my room would be command center where everyone stayed together until bedtime - met before meals and came to - in case of emergencies.

At 12:30 AM after everyone was asleep the fire alarm started going off. Tom and Mark were in our room immediately, dressed in pajamas, robes and slippers. Gene and I were dressed the same and all the people running down the hall were in similar attire. We had already called Bruce and Susan's room but they still were not in our room. The hallway emptied and we still waited for Bruce and Susan. Minutes more passed and they finally appeared - all dressed up in their Easter clothes. Bruce had even removed Susan's curlers and brushed her hair in ringlets.

145

We hurried out of the building and as we all stood outside on the sidewalk I couldn't help but notice that no one looked as nice as Bruce and Susan! Fortunately it was a false alarm - a sprinkler system on the roof had triggered the alarm.

Our visit with Reidun in Norway was marvelous. She was well adjusted and happy to see Gene. Her mother, aunt and uncle were charming and Michelle was a beautiful, almost six-year old. She and Susan had a great time together. The experiences we had in that beautiful country will always be with us, especially the one of the boating adventure that we had. Reidun was dating a very nice attorney and he made arrangements for all of us to go out for dinner in a memorable way. He had a friend who owned a fishing boat. Now the fishing boats in Norway are nothing like the ones I have seen in the United States - they are built of thick heavy timbers, as they were in the days of the Vikings, so the boat was massive, sturdy and rugged. It was a perfect afternoon for an outing, and we were all happy and excited as we boarded the boat with our buckets and baskets of food. We found places to stand and sit near the railing as the boat engine started and we putted away from our mooring and out of the harbor where we picked up speed and moved into the waters of the fiord.

We remarked at the expertise of our boat Captain as he skill-fully maneuvered the boat in a winding fashion between the gigantic rounded rocks that we could see just beneath the water's surface. We were leaving behind the activity and bustle of the busy little picturesque seaport with its marina, colorful flags and a variety of work and pleasure boats secured to the jutting piers. We traveled on and entered the wide passageway of boulders that loomed up on either side of us. As the mouth of the fiord widened, the rock wall became lower and we could see ahead where the rocks ended and the sea began.

Our captain, standing at the impressive wooden and brass wheel, used great dexterity and took us into a little cove where we were able to climb out and over the rocks with our food supplies. We gathered weathered wood and built a fire to heat a large kettle of water and cook the buckets of freshly caught shrimp that we brought with us. While the water

heated, we investigated our rocky playground and looked out at the open sea. By the time the water boiled and the shrimp were cooked we were ravenous. Everything tasted good but I especially remember the wonderful flavor of the shrimp after we each peeled our own, dipped it in communal bowls of either drawn butter or cocktail sauce, and ate it with chunks of fresh Norwegian bread. We ate pounds of shrimp there on those beautiful smooth rocks that looked almost white in contrast to the blue of the sky and the deeper blue of the water. What a wonderful dinner with delightful friends and family! It was fortunate that we brought paper towels and water to wash our hands and faces, because we were in dire need of them when we came to the bottom of the last bowl of shrimp.

After we dowsed the fire and spread out the last remaining embers, we packed up and started back to the boat. The steady sea breeze began to grow stronger and bear down on us as we went back aboard - our hair and clothing were whipping around us as if to give warning of something worse to come. Gigantic black clouds bounded through the sky butting the lazy, white puffy clouds over their heads and out of sight until they completely obliterated the brightness of the blue sky and the warmth of the sun. We were all amazed at the eerie racing movement in the sky, and our hearts quickened as the ferocious wind dug deep into the water and churned it up into heaving waves that made our rugged boat seem like a floating cork bobbing out of control. All I could envision were the countless rocks just under the water's surface that our captain had to avoid. The first heavy rain drops hit us like silver dollars falling from the sky, and then the fury of the storm was upon us. Piercing streaks of lightning lit up the sky, and rolling claps of thunder added their boisterous sounds to the raging storm, and by then the rain was falling in diagonal sheets.

Each of us clung to railings or whatever secure, stationary structure we could find. Gene had the younger children in a pro-tected area near the captain at the base of the ship's wheel until we could inch our way to the hatch and go below to the quar-ters, but once we were there, it was difficult to hold on to anything and we would get tossed across the room. It was easy to get seasick down there so some of us returned to

147

the deck to weather the storm. I kept praying for our safe return to land, and for the captain. He did a marvelous job! We all rejoiced when the storm started to subside and the boat became more stable. The rain reduced itself to a steady shower and the thunder rumbled in the distance as it moved begrudgingly away, taking the flashing lightning with it. They left us with a final grumble and only a few eruptions of light glimmering through the dark sky on the horizon. The last remaining raindrops were sparkling through the sunshine as the sky turned blue again. Everything glistened and even the air seemed so squeaky clean that you wanted to breathe it deeply.

From Norway we went by train to Copenhagen, Stockholm and Germany. In Celle, Germany we stayed with our dear friends, the Kruegers. They had been our friends in Virginia Beach where we lived near each other. Hans was a distinguished doctor and was chief resident surgeon at Norfolk General Hospital. We felt lost when they moved back to their homeland so it was good to renew our friendship with them. All too soon our memorable trip ended and we returned to our life back home.

THE PATCHWORK of MY LIFE

149

Chapter 21

The Bursting of a Balloon

In May all of the repatriated POW's were invited to the White House for dinner as guests of President and Mrs. Nixon. Each military service made special plans for the occasion. We stayed in a very nice hotel and a meeting with guest speakers was planned in the afternoon in a large conference room and after that, we would be given time enough to go to our rooms to get dressed in formal attire for the evening dinner. At the appropriated meeting time, Gene and I left our room to go down to the conference room. I was excited to see the wives again and finally meet their husbands. As we walked to the elevator I noticed how nice the men looked in their uniforms and Gene was especially handsome walking beside me holding my hand. When we got on the elevator, one of my dear friends from Virginia Beach was there with her husband. I beamed and stepped over to give her a hug but I sensed a strained awkwardness. I didn't quite understand what was going on. Gene and I found the conference room and went in. Part way down near the center I saw another wife I knew - we had roomed together on some of our

With all my love

trips to Washington. I led the way for Gene, went in the row and sat down beside her husband - she sat just beyond him and Gene sat down beside me. After speaking to my friend, I put out my hand to him and with a big smile I said, "Welcome Home," and I called him by name saying, "I have prayed for you so often that I feel as if I already know you." He smiled and responded warmly and then his wife introduced us. When he heard my name he glared at us, stood up, took his wife by the hand and they left. Gene and I sat alone in that middle row. The room filled with repatriated prisoners and their wives and a few people had to stand in the back of the room but they would not use the empty seats in our row. I tried to keep from trembling, I was crushed. Gene sat erect - holding my hand and I would have to hold my head up, too, but the tears slid down my cheeks. I didn't hear any of the speeches and while people mingled we quickly slipped out. I could not wait to be in the quiet sanctuary of our room. Gene unlocked the door and we went in to find that our room had been vandalized and the mirrors were covered with ugly words and phrases. I felt broken and wanted to cry but Gene started cleaning the mirrors and I put the room back in order. I didn't need to make people feel uncomfortable by talking to them when we went to the White House. I would just stay close to Gene and talk to him. Why were my hands so cold and still shaking? Lord, help me to forgive.

As it turned out we had a wonderful time at the White House. President and Mrs. Nixon stood at the door to welcome us and shake our hand when we arrived. They had invited so many celebrities that I can not even name them all: Bob Hope, John Wayne, Jimmy Stewart, Edgar Bergen and Charlie McCarthy, Phyllis Diller, Sammy Davis, Jr., Ricardo Montelban, Heads of State, Senators, etc. etc. The whole house was open to us - even the private quarters of the President. It was a rare privilege to walk wherever you chose without being part of a tour group. When they announced that dinner would be served we went to the Rose Garden where carpeting covered the lawn and canopies were overhead. The lighting was soft and beautiful and the round tables for eight were elegantly set. Flowers were everywhere. I grew concerned about our table partners. The seating arrangement had already been designated - place cards were at each setting.

151

Chapter 22

Gene's Story

On Father's Day 1968 Gene's Phantom II was hit by ground fire (this is what Gene believes and Em, his wingman, thought he was hit by a missile from a MIG). The plane was on fire and none of the controls were working, they were diving toward the ground and the ejection systems would not work. The F4J had a sophisticated system; when triggered, the canopies would fly off, the back seat would eject with the RIO and then the pilot's seat would eject with great force to lift them far from the damaged plane before the parachutes opened and took the men carefully to the ground. It was different with Gene and Bernie; when the ejection system did not work they knew it was each man for himself - even their radio went out and they could not talk to each other. After Gene made four varying attempts to make it work, he was convinced he was going to die as the jet screamed on fire out of the sky. Then he pulled one last manual lever and the canopy came off, then he pulled the face curtain. He was propelled up and away from the jet. The parachute takes 1-3/4 seconds to deploy once the ejection happens. The flaming plane crashed and exploded *before* the parachute opened, which means Gene's life was spared by less than 1/30th of a minute. We cannot think of the accident without grieving for Bernie who did not get out safely.

Gene landed in a deeply furrowed rice paddy and because of the rough terrain he severely sprained his left ankle. Ejection seat parachutes are not big and fancy like the ones you see at air shows - they are only 22' in diameter and have no controls. A group of North Vietnamese were firing at him from less than 100' away. Gene saw them running toward him while the parachute was still in the air so he knew there was no escape but he tried to hobble away and hide behind a scrawny tree

154

and some short grass. Gene cannot recall being able to make a broadcast on his radio because he was only on the ground for about one minute before he was captured. The Vietnamese knocked him to the ground by hitting him on the shoulder and neck with a large bamboo pole. Then they started removing his clothes. Gene was wearing many specialized items of flight gear - including a very heavy survival vest. When they started to cut through the laces on his flight boots, Gene could not stand to see them damaged so he put up his hand to gesture that he would unlace them and remove the boots. They took everything except his undershorts and T-shirt and handkerchief, which they used as a blindfold. They even took his watch, wedding ring, dog tags, ID card and Geneva Convention card.

It was very difficult for him to walk with the bad ankle and barefooted over the hard-stubbled roughness of the ground. They tied a rope around him and led him away. A small boy, like our Thomas, came and took his hand and led the way by indicating with a lift or a downward motion the rises and falls of the ground. Gene was impressed that this guidance kept Gene from stumbling and the small boy did not abandon him. (God sent an angel before I even prayed for one! Isn't He wonderful?) They took him to a small primitive house where he sat on a dirt floor in the corner of a room. He remembers a dog and children running around and he was given water from a rusty soup can. He was moved at night and stayed in similar dwellings each day.

A few nights later they started moving Gene by truck. His upper arms were tied behind him and he sat in the back of a dump truck filled with crushed rocks. The journey was extremely bumpy which caused great discomfort sitting on sharp rocks, barefooted and in his undershorts. The truck stopped abruptly and the Vietnamese ordered Gene out of the truck - using their rifle butts to prod him hurriedly to an underground shelter a few feet back from the edge of the road. Gene could hear a jet and as it flew closer, from his vantage point in the shelter, he saw a flare light the sky to the right of him and one to the left of him. As they lit up the sky Gene saw the parachute of an unlighted flare that had been dropped in the middle - directly over the truck. In the meantime - the plane had turned around and was

155

coming back in to attack the target with 750-pound bombs that are armed with instantaneous nose fuses, which means they don't penetrate the ground. As soon as they touch the ground they explode sending shrapnel hundreds of feet along the surface to destroy trucks, tanks and any material. Because the center flare did not light, the truck was not revealed. Gene had never seen a flare not work. He was spared again because their mission was to bomb the truck if they saw one. He knew the A6 pilot from the USS America. I am thankful God chose to protect Gene and not allow his friend to drop the bomb that would have probably taken his life.

On the seventh day Gene was riding in the back of another truck. It was daytime and extremely hot and he had not had water. As he sat on the hard surface with arms tied behind and his head on his knees under a canvas to hide him and keep him from seeing where he was going, he began to have strange sensations of vertigo. When the truck turned in one direction he thought he was doing an inside loop and when the truck turned in the other direction he would be in an outside loop. While it was happening he thought it was a fun sensation - it reminded him of flying.

He had a rude awakening when the truck arrived at the prison in downtown Hanoi. As soon as the truck stopped his guards were at the back of the truck using their rifle butts again and ordering him out of the truck. He tried to accommodate but something was wrong. When he tried to stand he could not maintain his balance. Gene scooted himself to the back of the truck and they assisted him to the ground. When they realized he could not stand they half carried him into the building. With their help he could walk but he had no sense of balance and could not stand alone.

Gene was taken to a large room that would be his home for nearly two weeks - the only furnishings were a small desk, a wooden chair and a little stool about 10 inches high. The stool was for the prisoner to sit on while he was being interrogated but Gene could not sit on it, he couldn't even sit on the floor - he had to crawl to a corner and using the two walls as a brace he could sit. Sometimes he tried to sit against the wall but eventually would slide over to the floor.

They brought Gene his first meal and he realized that his mouth didn't work - the food came out the left side so he learned to hold his left lips with his hand while he chewed. That night he discovered that his left eye would not close but if he used his fingers to pull his eyelid down it would stay closed. As he tried to analyze this problem that made him feel like he had an extra large shot of Novocain - even to the numbed, thick tongue on the left side of his mouth - he realized that the left side of his face was paralyzed. He also discovered that the right side of his torso did not feel correct. Temperature felt like pressure and pressure felt like temperature - if he pressed the floor with his hand - it felt hot.

When the camp commander came in to interrogate - Gene was able to convince him that Gene had a problem with paralysis and the camp commander sent a man to give Gene vitamin shots for seven days (the Vitamin smelled like B12). Gene was grateful they only asked him a few insignificant questions. As he lay in that room going through the misery of making his body work again he faced another challenge - he began to think about the appropriateness of our involvement.

Gene's next room was a small cell only 3-1/2' x 8' and the ceiling was 15' above him. High up on the wall was a portion of an open window where all he could see, as he looked up to see through it, was a stone wall about 20' high with barbed wire and jagged pieces of broken glass on top. His bed, made from two mahogany planks about 2-1/2 inches thick, took up most of his room, but he was not allowed to lie down on it except during sleeping time. He was given a black pajama-like uniform, sandals made from rubber tires, two blankets, a small hand-sized towel which would serve as wash cloth, bath towel, napkin and handkerchief; a cup with lid, a tooth brush, tooth paste, a piece of soap, several pieces of toilet paper and a waste bucket with a cover on it. He had no clock, calendar, paper, pencil, book, mirror, comb, nail-clipper or anything similar that we would think of as necessities. This cell was where Gene lived for twenty-two months in solitary confinement - completely isolated from other Americans - he never heard the tapping messages they talk about now. At first he could only eat, sleep and exercise to regain the use of his ankle -

157

which took nine months and it took a year to recover from the paralysis with a few lingering effects that remained until he had been home a few years.

Gene spent much time planning and renovating our home and he built several homes. First he visualized the finished product and then he drew an exact plan in his mind. He figured the amount of building supplies that would be required and then he constructed the home in proper order. It was like going to work - each day he began where he left off the day before. He spent hours thinking about words and their meanings, Bible verses, oaths he had taken or made. Never before had he been given so much time to think. One day he became very discouraged and could not even go to work on the house he was building. He sat . . . and finally asked God for something - anything to take up his time. From the open window a ray of sunlight shone into his cell and when he looked up, a tiny, downy feather was floating down through the sunlight. He waited for it to come into his reach and holding out his open palm, the little feather landed, bounced and danced in his hand. After studying it he blew it up in the air again and it would gently fall back to his hand. He played with God's feather for a long time.

But the war would not go away.

There he was, a twenty-plus year Naval officer, wondering why the United States Congress had never declared war in Vietnam and why the United Nations had never sanctioned our presence there. He said, "I thought about it and prayed about it and tried to find some appropriate reason to continue the war." It kept bothering him but he did not want to make a decision. No matter how he rationalized he could find no legal basis for the war but he felt "stupid" to have been fighting a war and then turn around and say it was wrong. He knew he was a minority and thought that must mean he was wrong but every day he tested his new beliefs and could not find anything wrong with them so he decided he was in a minority but he was right.

While Gene was in solitary confinement he contracted hepatitis and became very jaundiced. At one point the Vietnamese treated it by giving him bananas - sometimes he had as many as 16 a day. The bananas and his constant exercising paid off and he improved quickly.

Gene continued pondering the war and finally decided that he had to speak out. One of the oaths he had gone over in his mind at the very beginning of his internment was his Loyalty Oath "to obey the *legal* orders of all those appointed over him" which means an order must be legal to be obeyed. Gene, like everyone else, was not a volunteer in Vietnam, he was ordered there which means the order that sent them there had to have a legal basis and it had to come from the official rendering of the Constitution of the United States. The Constitution requires that Congress declares war and they had not done that.

Gene has told me that he never had special treatment that was not available to others. He only received 22 of my letters and he was there 23 months before he received his first letter from me. When they left the prison, many men had belongings returned to them including their wedding rings; but Gene did not get his ring or anything else back. Gene was not tortured but much of the torture had stopped by the time he was captured in 1968, besides, we were constantly praying for his safety and is it possible that God allowed the stroke - to protect him? Gene realizes that the stroke made him less aggressive... Gene found that when he was asked difficult questions during interrogation that his reply of, "Would you give out information that would harm your country if you were in my place?" brought favorable results and the reason it worked is because the North Vietnamese were very nationalistic.

Unless you know Gene you cannot begin to realize the depth of his devotion and compassion for his country. He believes that our Constitution is the most perfect document that any country in the world has been able to conceive and he will fight for its principles as long as he lives. How could anyone think that he would act in a traitorous way? Gene has admitted that it would be easier if we could just be Jeanne Wilber, wife and mother; and Gene Wilber, husband and father, but he cannot let go of his concerns for our country.

Those are a few of the things I was thinking about that summer when the charges were made against Gene. The possibility of court martial was almost inconceivable to me. How could I protect his honor? Gradually the flow of support started up again; friends from my college town formed a Concerned Citizens Committee and they sent out petitions and letters. Our family and friends remained true, other communities expressed concern or support and the summer passed by. Our faith in God was made stronger as we prayed to love and pray for our enemies and with His help we learned to forgive.

Three months later the charges were dropped by Secretary of the Navy, John Warner. He was speaking in Towanda, PA soon after that and one of the people in the audience questioned Secretary Warner about the charges against Gene. The Secretary praised our family and said he hoped we could find happiness - we had suffered enough. We had not been in Towanda when he spoke but his remarks were printed in our local newspapers and we appreciated his kind words.

Oh, precious Lord - thank You for getting us through another trial. When will I ever reach the point that James (1:2-3) talks about: "Consider it all joy — *when* you encounter various trials, knowing that the testing of your faith produces endurance?" Forgive me, Lord, that I did not stop to consider it all joy *when* the charges were made and help me to remember, in the future, that trials produce endurance *when* they happen, not later as You send friends to build us up. Thank You for another example that confirms that You are in control and thank You for letting us realize more than ever that our hope and trust are in You. Thank You for working things out for good, we *do* love You!

Sweeter as the Years Go By

Lelia N. Morris, 1862-1929

Lelia N. Morris, 1862-1929

1. Of Je - sus' love that sought me When I was lost in sin —
2. He trod in old Ju - de - a Life's path - way long a - go —
3. 'Twas won - drous love which led Him For us to suf - fer loss —

Of won - drous grace that brought me Back to His fold a - gain —
The peo - ple thronged a - bout Him His sav - ing grace to know;
To bear with - out a mur - mur The an - guish of the cross;

Of heights and depths of mer - cy Far deep - er than the sea
He healed the bro - ken-heart - ed And caused the blind to see;
With saints re - deemed in glo - ry Let us our voic - es raise,

And high - er than the heav - ens, My theme shall ev - er be.
And still His great heart yearn - eth In love for e - ven me.
Till heav'n and earth re - ech - o With our Re - deem - er's praise.

CHORUS

Sweet - er as the years go by, Sweet - er as the years go by;
Sweet - er as the years go by, 'Tis sweet - er as the years go by;

Rich - er, full - er, deep - er, Je - sus' love is sweet - er, Sweet - er as the years go by.

PART THREE

"SWEETER AS THE YEARS GO BY"

Chapter 23

The Family

Where do the years go? As I look back now, it seems that the time Gene was in prison went by at a snails pace while the years that followed zoomed by like a race car on a speedway. Maybe the old sayings are true; "time flies when you're having fun" or "the older you grow the faster time goes." Even though the black cloud of the charges against Gene hung over both of us that summer, we made sure life went on very normally in our family. The children loved having their Dad home. We took long walks across our fields and through our woods, and planted our garden. Tom graduated from high school in early June and was going on to Penn State in September. Bruce was up high on a cloud! He met Linda Balmer when he was 17 and came home to tell me he met the girl he wanted to marry. Her parents were old friends of ours. Bruce and Linda saw each other for awhile but then Bruce went off to Alfred University in New York State. One and one-half years later when Gene was released from prison Linda wrote a beautiful letter to Bruce expressing her happiness for him and saying their prayers had been answered. I took special note of Bruce that day. He was always comfortable having all of us around - if he got mail he sat down in the family room to read it while we were present, but when he recognized Linda's writing he went upstairs, three steps at a time, and sat on his bed (I know because Susan ran after him and told me what was going on) to read the letter. He called Linda that day and by early summer they came to us and said they would like to get married. We talked to them about waiting - they were only 19 but they were in love and we were happy for them. The wedding was on September 22, 1973. Linda was a wonderful addition to our family and now they are still happily married and have John (26), Joe (24) and Summer (22) who is married to Mat Berry and they have two sons - Cole (3) and Luke (1) (our wonderfully special great-grandsons).

In October 1973, Gene retired from the Navy. Of the 25-1/2 years he was in the service, 18-1/2 years were spent on sea duty. It had been a wonderful life for us but I was thankful to know that we would be together for the rest of our lives. We did not know what was ahead because at 43, Gene was too young to retire but we knew God would be with us, guiding and directing and we would be following.

Hard as it was to have Tom leave for college - we en-

Bruce & Linda

Joe, John & Summer

Cole & Luke

Mat, Summer & Cole

THE PATCHWORK of MY LIFE

joyed his weekends at home and we loved going to State College to visit him, go to football games and meet his friends. Mark and Susan were happy to leave for school knowing their Dad would be there when they came home. Our first Christmas together seemed more like Thanksgiving than Christmas. Gene was home, Bruce and Linda had gone to Wills Eye Hospital in Philadelphia where Bruce had a successful cornea transplant in November, Tom was home for the holidays, Mom was with us and Mark and Susan were happily involved in everything we planned and did.

Mom was with us a great deal but holidays were difficult for her. After the excitement of Gene's return wore off and we were not traveling back and forth to the Philadelphia Naval Hospital; even though we spent every Sunday with Mom, took her grocery shopping each week, called her every morning, and had her over for dinner three to five times a week; she felt cut off. Mom had spent every day, after we left Virginia Beach, with the children and me while Gene was gone. She had stopped teaching the month before the children and I moved up here and then when we arrived she came over at 8:00 nearly every morning and left at 10:30 or 11:00 at night. We were happy to have her with us but I was fearful of the changes that would be brought about in her life when Gene came home; so I prayed about something to help fill the gap in her life. Mom was an antique collector and was very knowledgeable so the children and I gradually began talking to her about starting an Antique Shop in one of her out buildings. We all helped empty it and she became very interested in it but not interested enough to set up regular hours and stay home. Saturday became her day to stay home and we took her to church every Sunday and then went back to her home for lunch, so Sunday afternoon turned out to be a good business day because her customers knew they could find her there. And now it was winter, and Gene was home and Mom's favorite saying became, "I live alone, I don't have a soul." It hurt to have her repeatedly tell me that when she had more people around her than anyone else I knew. She was only 64 and her home was the haven for countless people; antique dealers and customers loved to sip tea and sit in the wing chairs by her fireplace and talk with her. She was a Justice of the Peace and Notary so the State Troopers made daily visits with her while they sat at the kitchen table drinking coffee. Relatives kept close track of her and came to visit or play cards; friends loved being with her. She was involved in the Elmira Button Club and Pauline went up to call on her late in the evening to carry in wood for her fire and see if she had any needs before she went to bed. Gene was faithful to do her banking every Monday morning and to keep up with general repairs and maintenance around her home. Bruce and Linda truly loved her and either had her for dinner in their home or went to hers as often as they could.

Gene and I spent the winter months of 1974 talking and drawing plans for an addition on our home and we still had a great deal to share about the five years we were separated. Much as we loved our home, it had a very small kitchen and no dining room, utility room or garage. On the days I baked our weekly batch of nine loaves of bread and was trying to can garden produce, it was difficult to find space to cook a meal. The meals were big - our home always seemed to attract our children's

Enjoying each other

friends. I loved and enjoyed the extra people around the table. Because Mom was here Aunt Ruth and Uncle Bob or Aunt Louise and Uncle Brownie were here frequently. Summers were easy because we could all eat outside on picnic tables but winters took some balancing so the plans for a new large kitchen made me very excited. The addition would be 32' x 52' and would have a kitchen, dining room, walk in pantry, bathroom, utility room, double garage and stairway leading up to a 16' x 52' loft which would house a ping pong table and be a hobby, recreation

and herb and onion drying room for the family and later be a good place for youth and church groups to meet.

In April we broke ground and though we hired some carpenters - Gene, Mark, Susan and I worked all that summer on the addition and did the inside finishing work through the winter of 74/75. It was completed in March 1975 and what fun it was to move in, get it settled and cook our first meal! One of the things Gene, Mark, Susan and I enjoyed building most in the addition was the large stone kitchen fireplace. Every evening after our day's work was done we would go off with Mark, Susan and I, sitting in the trailer of our little tractor, while Gene drove to unused parts of our land and we searched for weathered field stones with "character." We looked for them so often that when we closed our eyes at night we saw large stones and rock. We needed tons because we had to build a 27' high outside chimney also. When we found rocks too large to lift, Gene and Mark would go back after them with our big tractor and loader. We found a man in a town about 30 miles away who owned a quarry and he let the four of us go there to quarry our own stone. We had such exciting happy times doing it! Mark took metal shop in 8th grade and made an iron crane for the fireplace. Working on the addition was not only rewarding to us because of the final results, but it also was an invaluable learning experience for Mark and Susan. They have an innate knowledge of construction and though all four of our children had always worked with us, kept their bedrooms clean and had chores to do - this experience taught them even more about good work ethics.

As if the addition was not enough to think about, during the summer of 1974 we went to a registered Angus auction in Virginia and bought our first eleven beef cattle. They were beautiful animals. We had been thinking and talking about buying some registered Angus and we went to this auction just to get some ideas and *look* at the animals - we had no intention of buying but then we didn't know how appealing these girls would be. We were totally unprepared - we didn't even have a fenced in area. We drove our motor home back home, borrowed a cattle truck from a friend and went back after the animals. When we brought them home they had to wait on the truck while we quickly set up an electric fence. They were happy with their small

167

green pasture but they certainly ate it up quickly. We worked diligently ahead of them to build fences, buy watering tubs and get in gear to be beef cattle farmers. By the next spring we had 35.

In December 1974, John Michael was born - our first grandson and what a beautiful treasure he was! Christmas was especially easy to celebrate that year when we could all take turns holding that precious little boy!

When Gene returned from Hanoi the doctors discovered a thyroid deficiency and they prescribed Synthroid for him to take daily. The doctors thought it might have been caused by eating only cabbage for such a long time. (In the early days of Oklahoma the settlers grew fields and fields of cabbage. Because their diets consisted of mostly cabbage and they did not have iodized salt, the people started to develop goiters.) As time went on Gene's thyroid problem worsened and by the winter of 1976 when he went to Pensacola, Florida for his annual physical, the doctors wanted to operate while he was there because he was hardly able to swallow. Gene said he wanted me to be with him so he flew home and we drove down to Bethesda Naval Hospital. When they operated they discovered that his thyroid had grown to the size of a small grapefruit and it was very vascular (filled with blood). They removed it and sent it to Pathology where it was learned that the thyroid was malignant. The doctor felt that it had been growing since Gene was hit in the neck with the bamboo pole at the time he was captured. Gene spent the rest of that winter recuperating and we had to sell our herd of 66 Black Angus.

"All is well that ends well" though, because Gene was called and asked if he would be the pilot for a charter flight service at a local airport. It was a different experience to be flying the Piper Navajo and Cherokee instead of jets, but he really enjoyed his new job as well as the daily routine of going to work and being in and around the hangar.

That year our second grandson, Joe Bruce, was born on September 27, 1976 - another beautiful grandson and so much fun to be around! By that time Bruce and Linda had bought their first home. It was a nice little ranch style with a few acres of land and a separate place for Bruce to start his

*Susan on Candy
with Bruce*

*Mark &
Buttercup*

own used car business. The garage was large with office space, a space to work on cars and do body work and painting. Bruce loved being on his own and it was handy to be able to walk home whenever he wanted. Susan loved being with them and quite often Linda would invite her down - they only lived about eight miles from us.

Mark and Susan got involved in 4-H and Mark bought a Jersey calf. He named her Buttercup and we all enjoyed watching him show her at the Troy Fair. Mark and Susan enjoyed those years. Mark had Buttercup to care for and Susan had a pony.

Tom prepared to study dentistry but during his senior year he called us early one morning and said he wanted to go into the ministry. Of course, I was thankful and happy with his decision. In October of 1976 he and Linda Burkey became engaged. Linda and Tom had met at Linda's church in State College. Linda was a pretty, quiet woman who worked as a secretary. She had graduated with honors from South Hills Business School and worked at the Pennsylvania Fish Commission

169

at Benner Springs. Tom used to ride his road bike from campus all the way to the Fish Hatchery to visit her.

Tom graduated from Penn State the following spring and they were married on July 1, 1977. One sweet memory I have of their wedding ceremony was when Tom and Linda went forward to kneel in prayer and all of the wedding party remained in their places except their ring bearer, John who was 2-1/2 years old. Just as the minister was about to pray John put his pillow down, ran up to the kneeling bench and snuggled in between them. He looked so sincere as he bowed his head with them and his smile was radiant when he held his Uncle Tom's hand as they returned to the altar. That August they moved to Dayton, Ohio where Tom started his studies at United Theological Seminary for his Master's in Divinity.

Still at fast pace the years went by and Mark graduated from high school in June of '78. A few days *before* graduation he started college at Penn State. Perhaps because I didn't have him home that last summer after he finished high school to prepare myself for his leaving; I had a very hard time when he left - he seemed so young and then his first roommate was from Philadelphia and did not have the same standards that Mark had. I prayed hard for Mark that summer. He came home often and with some Christian friends got involved in Campus Crusade for Christ. From then on he was excited about his schooling and so was I. And again our home became a retreat center for his friends, as it had been for Tom and his friends when he was a student at Penn State.

And now Susan, Gene and I were together and what a joy she was and is to me! Susan and I loved doing the same things so having her around was always easy - especially in the kitchen. She was like an extension of me - never in the way and always adding to the pleasure.

In June 1978, Summer Lin, our first granddaughter was born and what a beauty she was and still is! She added her own special joy to the family and Bruce and Linda were such good parents to their three children - they always did fun things together!

In the winter of 1979 Gene had to have radiation at Bethesda Naval Hospital to deactivate all remaining thyroid. During that same period of time Mark and Susan started going to a church in their school district where many of their friends attended - two of the girls were the Pastor's daughters. It was an active little country church and they loved it there. Gene and I were very involved in our church - he was Chairman of the Administrative Board and I had been directing Christmas cantatas there since the children and I moved back to Pennsylvania. We loved all the people there because I knew them from my teenage years when I walked to that church every Sunday. Gene and I talked and felt it was not right for our children to go in one direction on Sunday and we go in the other. As soon as Gene finished his radiation we went to the Austinville Union Church for the first time and we felt at home. We already knew many of the members and as we sat through and participated in that service with Mark and Susan singing in the beautiful choir, we felt we belonged there. I had that joyous tingly feeling that let me know that God was

saying, "This is the right House." Gene is a deacon there and I am still directing cantatas each year with 50 to 60 wonderful friends to work with - they keep me young.

As Susan grew older she wanted everyone to call her Sue - just as Tom outgrew Thomas. Before we knew it in 1980 Sue was graduating from high school and by that time Gene had been on the school board for a few years; so he gave her the diploma and what a pretty sight that was to me. Sue went to my alma mater in Mansfield in the fall - I was glad she was only 12 miles away.

Sue graduating

171

Matthew, Tom, Linda, & Chris

Tom graduated from United Theological Seminary in 1980 and had done very well. He was accepted at Princeton to get his PhD but they moved home that summer and the owner of a local business came to see him. The business was in the red and he asked if Tom would be manager to see if Tom could give the business some life and get it in the black. Tom started working there and loved it. The business flourished! Next Tom worked as a counselor at a drug and alcohol abuse treatment center, but then he decided to join the Navy. He became a Supply Officer and had an outstanding career. He enjoyed his experiences of an assignment on the nuclear sub - the USS City of Corpus Christi — and also an assignment aboard the aircraft carrier USS Theodore Roosevelt. Eight years after they were married Tom and Linda had a son, Matthew. It had been seven years since we had a baby in the family

so we were excited and Matthew was so special: bright, warm and affectionate and he learned to recognize every different kind of car before he could even talk. Two years later Chris was born and he captured our hearts with his

Matthew

After a piano recital

Demonstrating their soccer techniques

winsome smile. He was a born winner and as he grew he developed a tenacious desire to excel. They were both wonderful babies and are exceptional young men today. They love soccer, track, basketball, studies, youth group, drums and are outstanding piano players. While Tom was in the Navy he went back to Penn State and earned his MBA. Then he was assigned to Mechanicsburg, PA which is the logistics center for the U. S. Navy. He worked hard there and the whole family enjoyed their years living on the base at Mechanicsburg. He resigned from the Navy as a Lieutenant Commander in 1996 and moved back home - he did not want to be gone during the boys' teenage years. Now Tom is a manager at Corning Incorporated. They live across the road from us in the building that Gene built for my business. After I retired in 1996, we changed it into a three-bedroom home. Tom and Linda bought it with some additional land and it is a great comfort to have them nearby.

I particularly enjoy them during the spring, summer and fall when we all spend more time outdoors. Linda and I can talk back and forth with each other while we weed our flower beds near the dirt road and we like to exchange multiplying plants. Matthew practices his soccer techniques and he amazes me as I watch his expertise and agility. Chris enjoys flying one of the motorized radio controlled airplanes that he and Tom have constructed, or both boys practice shooting baskets. Tom enjoys biking, swimming and he is a marathon runner.

173

I was especially happy to have him so close two years ago. One April night Rebecca called us between 9:30 and 10:00 PM to tell us she was concerned about a pickup truck that was speeding up and down our road and spending time up at Mark's offices. We had heard it but were not aware that Mark was not up there with Rebecca and the children. He was working quite a few miles away. Our dirt road dead ends at the edge of our pines just beyond Mark's office so traffic is a novelty to us and cause for alarm when anyone is acting erratically. Gene said he would go outside to check for her. As he went out I saw Tom's car pulling out of their driveway and I assumed Tom was taking his car up to put it in his barn as he does every night. Rebecca called back and said they were on their way back down again and my heart was in my mouth for fear they would crash into Tom so I said a quick prayer. Gene was standing at the end of our driveway making an up and down motion with his hand for them to slow down as the truck came flying down the hill. When they saw Gene they forcefully applied their brakes. Swerving, skidding and kicking up dust and gravel they came to a grinding halt at the foot of our dirt road. Because of our tall lilac bushes along the stone wall I lost my vantage point of the corner where the truck had stopped from the window where I was watching. I kept assuring myself that once Gene talked to them and calmed them down everything would be all right - why should I ever suspect a problem here in our peaceful community? My attempt to quell my concern was not convincing so I stepped out on the porch and realized that Tom's car was behind their truck - his door was wide open and the interior light was on. The noises I heard were chilling - thuds, yelling, brawling and blows being struck. As I became fearful for Gene and Tom I ran down the walk toward the stone steps that lead to the corner yelling, "Gene are you alright?" He painfully responded, "No." I could hear Tom running from his house. By the time I reached the top of the stone steps the three men jumped in the truck and fled.

When I thought Tom was driving his car to the barn he was, instead, on his way to investigate. He had been alarmed by the truck's speed and recklessness. They forced Tom off the road as they came down the hill and by the time he quickly turned his car around and pulled up behind them at the foot of the hill he saw them beating up his Dad. When Tom stopped his car and jumped out to help Gene, one of the men jumped on Tom from behind and kicked or slugged him in the back in his kidney area. Two more men had Gene in the ditch kicking him when Tom ran to his house and called the State Police. That is when I ran down the walk. I helped Gene in the house and Tom was going to take off after the truck but he came running up to say one of the men had taken the keys from his ignition so he pushed his car across the main road to our parking lot and ran up to his barn to get their other car and he left to find them.

As soon as I checked Gene over I called Linda and had her come over with the boys - I knew how frightened they were about Tom and I called Rebecca to update her. Then I cleaned Gene's wounds. He was badly bruised and his glasses were smashed. They had kicked him in the back in his kidney also - that seemed to be their quick method of immobilizing the victim. We were fortunate that Gene didn't require stitches and had no broken teeth but he was a sorry sight and was very sore and lame. We opted for him to go to his doctor the following morning because we were concerned about Tom and did not want to leave the house. We waited for the State Police to come. We had no idea where Tom was. Rebecca had reached Mark on his cell phone and he was on his way home.

Finally, Tom returned, having successfully located the offenders. As a submariner, Tom had conducted countless searches finding Soviet submarines in the silent depths of the oceans, so he figured he could find a pickup truck with a five-minute head start. Tom shut his car off at the next hill and listened. He saw the truck going up Coryland hill and followed it. They seemed unsuspecting because they were driving at a below normal rate of speed until they turned off Coryland Road onto Thunder Road and Tom followed. They stopped abruptly, jumped out of the truck and before Tom could put his car in reverse and back up they were all over his car pounding on the windshield and windows and trying to open his locked doors but he sped backwards and lost them. When he reached Coryland Road he made the pretense of driving toward home but then he turned his lights off, turned around and went up Thunder Road again. It was very hard to see. He went around a curve and suddenly stopped short.

175

A few yards ahead in the middle of the road, was the pickup truck on its side. They had been in such a wild rush to get away from Tom that they flipped over. Tom came back home to call the State Police and tell them where the truck was.

By this time Mark had returned home so he went with Tom back to the scene and when they arrived the truck was gone. They searched the area and up a side road they saw a suspicious-looking trailer - perhaps because it was so brightly lit up when all of the other homes they had passed looked so sleepy at that late hour. Mark remained in the car while Tom went to the door and knocked. A woman opened it and when Tom asked about the men she said she didn't know anything about them. Tom suspected she was not being entirely truthful so as he left he studied the vehicles parked outside and found the truck.

Tom and Mark went back the short distance to Thunder Road where the Stewarts live. They are the kind of Christian neighbors anyone would pray to have nearby in the middle of a nightmarish night. Mark had been best friends with their son in elementary school. From the Stewarts Tom called the State Police again and they arrived soon after that. The State Police went to the trailer, found the men and apprehended them. Another State Trooper came here to get a report from Gene. By then it was 1:00 AM.

If Tom had not been so persistent we would never have known where the truck went or who the men were and we would have never experienced the end result in God's plan. A hearing was set in the court of our local Magistrate a few days later and we started praying. The three of us prayed separately about it and all came to the same conclusion. We felt washed of animosity toward them and fervently wanted the experience to change their lives. During the two court hearings Gene and Tom were able to convey their forgiving attitude and in conversations afterward the men realized we were praying for them and they were sincerely sorry for the trouble they had caused.

Mark graduated from Penn State in 1982 with a degree in Agronomy. His years of working with his Dad to get our fields back in order and then his summer jobs work-

176

ing at a big nursery, truck farm, produce business near Elmira gave him a special interest in agriculture. Though some good job opportunities came up, Mark was able to take an added concentrated college course. At that time Pennsylvania provided a one-time grant program to train a select group of recent Pa. State University graduates in the use of emerging micro computer science, accounting and business management skills and after that he started in business for himself as a Systems Analyst. After he graduated from Penn State he renewed a friendship with the daughter of friends of ours. He had known her when she was about eleven when our two families had dinner together but he had not seen her until we were invited to their home for dinner again in 1982. Lo and behold, this Rebecca Prutsman was a lovely young woman! They spent the whole evening talking to each other and they started dating immediately. That Christmas was very special. Mark shared his plan with us and believe me he had gone into this

Rebecca & Mark

relationship very prayerfully. On Christmas Eve we invited Rebecca and her parents, Tom and Nancy and brother Eric, up for the evening and Mark asked Rebecca if she wanted to go for a little drive. He took her up to our pines where we had a cleared area for bonfires. Mark had gone up earlier and built a fire and placed a log nearby for them to sit on. When they arrived the mood was perfect and the fire was flickering. As they sat watching it he proposed to her, she said "Yes!"; he placed

177

her diamond on her finger and they prayed together. They came down the hill so excited and sat on the floor in the family room where we were visiting. Rebecca kept flashing her ring and it took forever for her parents to notice! They were married on July 2, 1983.

After Rebecca was graduated with a BS degree in Exceptional Persons (Special Education) from Mansfield University, they moved to Tallahassee, Florida where her brother, Eric, was pursuing a Juris Doctorate at Florida State College of Law. Rebecca taught school in Georgia and Mark started his computer business but fortunately for us they decided to move back to Pennsylvania and they started build-

Rebecca, Mark, Isaac, Maryah,
Mattea & Andrew

ing on our land. They built a charming small house where they lived for a few years and then they built a beautiful Post and Beam saltbox home next to it. Now the little house is called the Pantry where they do their certified organic food processing. Their grains are stored there and they have a stone ground flour mill. Recently they bought the adjoining farm and use that home for Mark's offices. He owns or manages several different businesses which include LPW & Associates LLC (that was the original computer business and now they do internet development), RCW Publishing Co., Mulberry Development Group, which is a real estate business and he farms 123 acres of certified organic land. Their children are: Andrew (1989) who has a spirit of obedience with a desire to please. He is a deep thinker and has a creative imagination. Mattea (1993) is a thoughtful, caring, compassionate and tender hearted girl. Isaac (1995) means laughter and it fits him perfectly - he has an innate wit that puts a smile

178

on your face! Maryah (1997) is a sweet cherub and a delight to everyone. Gene and I are fortunate and thankful to have them living next door where they can come down often to put an added spark in our lives and keep us intertwined in their precious lives. It has given us the opportunity to observe how much they respect, protect and care for each other which makes for an atmosphere of sweet peace and harmony. Rebecca home schools their chil-

Mark and Rebecca just went to China to pick up their adopted daughter in October, 2001. Here she is!! We love her already.

dren and involves them in outside activities: church, piano lessons, karate and other seasonal projects. I am thankful Rebecca stays physically fit by walking every day. During good weather she goes in the early afternoon with Maryah in the racing stroller so she can take her nap. Andrew, Mattea and Isaac walk as far as my garden and stay with me. Sometimes Andrew paces around me telling me an interesting story while I weed or he and Isaac catch Japanese beetles while Mattea and I solve some of the deep issues of living a life that is pleasing to Jesus. I always have a stone bucket near the garden path and Isaac is a very good stone picker. Soon

Mark and Rebecca will be going to China to get a baby girl they are in the process of adopting and we all await that happy day when we can welcome Mishala into the family.

Andrew, Isaac, Mattea, Mishala & Maryah

In May 1985, Sue told me that she, at 23, had decided she would never get married. The following weekend she went alone to Elmira for "Arts in the Park." She walked from booth to booth looking at the works of local artists and was attracted to the sound of music. Following the rhythmic beat she came to a stage set up for "cloggers." As she stood there watching she didn't notice the second young man to her right nudge the first young man to her right and ask him to talk to her. You would have to know Donnie to appreciate this conversation because he is intelligent, professional and a perfect gentleman. He could not think of anything very intelligent or professional to say, so he asked Sue, "What are they doing?" Sue looked a little puzzled and said "Dancing." It did open a door though and Sue met the four very nice young men beside her and felt comfortable with them. They had a sandwich together before she came home.

Sue told me that one of the young men (the second from the right) was named Marc Efthimiou and they were all from Spencer, NY. Sue said Marc wanted to come Monday evening to visit her and meet us. For years Sue had asked me to pray about the young man that was "right" for her and whenever she dated someone she would ask me what I thought about him. Some I thought could always be her good friend and some I did not think she should continue seeing, but I never said "He is the right one." I prayed about this Marc before he arrived. Gene and I were in the garden that evening and Sue walked around front to greet him when he drove in the driveway. They came to the back of the house and walked down the garden path. When I stood to welcome him I loved him immediately - it was as if he had a glow around him (when I told that to Gene afterward he laughed and said I was light-headed because I just stood up). Marc was such a gentleman and had a warm and natural smile when he introduced himself as he shook our hands. He was very easy to talk to and his special qualities of gentleness and kindness were apparent. Not only was he nice, he also was a Cornell graduate and was an engineer at IBM. (Now please don't get me wrong - I didn't pounce on him and I did not let Sue know how I felt. I wanted to give it some time and see how Sue felt about him.) Two weeks later (after they had seen each other nearly every evening)

Sue and I were cooking dinner and she asked me what I thought about Marc. I told her I needed to know her feelings before I expressed mine and she told me that she felt that she really loved him. I told her about my experience in the garden and as I continued to pray for them God only made me feel more convinced that Marc and Sue were "right" for each other. A few weeks later Marc wanted to talk to Gene so Sue and I excused ourselves and went to Gene's and my bedroom but we (I'm ashamed to say) stood near the door to listen and when we heard Marc ask Gene for Sue's hand in marriage, Sue and I were (in suppressed silence) jumping up and down hugging each other! Gene called us and we quickly put on innocent, unknowing expressions and walked in the family room where Gene told us what Marc had said. When Gene asked me what I thought I just hugged them both!

Sue & Marc with Pastor Ken Marple

They were married on December 21, 1986. Not long after that Marc went back to Cornell to get his MBA and while he was doing well there, Cornell Law School sent him an invitation. After some prayer he entered law school and

181

got both degrees. After he graduated he took a position with Sullivan & Cromwell in New York City and worked as an international corporate attorney. It was a promising position and they loved their home, their church family and their neighborhood in Chatham, NJ; but Marc worked long hours and traveled out of the country frequently. He loved his work but realized he was seldom home when the children were awake so he took a position with a law firm in Elmira where they lived for about three years. Then Corning Inc. asked him to join their legal team. Now they live in the country near Corning, NY (22 miles from us) in a large Victorian home with 100 acres of land where Sue home schools their children. They have a large garden and plenty of space for their children to play and explore.

Marc and Sue with their six children

Marc and Sue have six beautiful children. Rachael (1989) was an alert and precocious baby and now we can add competent, responsible and outgoing to that list. She is an excellent violin and piano player and she has two younger sisters (Anna and Mikaela) following her love for music. They play violin and piano and Daniel also plays the piano. Daniel (1992) is gentle and affectionate with a winning smile. He loves sports and is very easy to please. Anna (1993) [her full name is Christianna Victoria] has a sparkling personality, an exuberant zest for life and is full of

laughter. Mikaela (1995) started studying people when she was just a baby. She is a little shy but once you capture her heart she is your loving friend for life. Abram (1998) is loving and bright with great confidence. He works and plays with boundless energy. From spring to fall they all help with the garden and work like little beavers at it. Sue makes it fun for them and they enjoy working with her. Daniel keeps it nicely cultivated with an antique push cultivator. Rachael and Anna help plant, weed or pick - whatever the seasonal need may be and Mikaela and Abram enjoy watering with the hose (sometimes they get an irresistible urge to make a little mud hole and sit down to make mud pies). During the summer they have a produce stand in their circular driveway and sell organic produce and herbs. On special occasions they post a sign giving the time for a Violin Concert. Each of these five children are unique and wonderful and now they have a baby sister that will strengthen and bless them in ways they can not imagine!

On October 11, 2000 Sue had a doctor's appointment. There was concern because the baby was either transverse or it would move to a breach position and it was due within a day or two. They did an ultrasound and the technician did some measuring while the doctor was talking. Sue saw the look of apprehension when the technician looked at the doctor and finally the doctor said, "Your baby's femur is short which could mean any of three things: it could be a Down syndrome baby, it could be a dwarf or it could be a normal short legged baby." Sue had not wanted her third Caesarian because Marc had a herniated disc at that time and Sue needed to be able to get right back to her many duties at home. The doctor told Sue that if the baby came rump first there would probably be room for the shoulders and head but if it came feet first he feared there might be a delay getting the shoulders and head out which could cause problems. The doctor wanted Sue in the hospital the next day. Sue's doctor delivered three of her babies so the nurses and technician had become Sue's friends and they were very concerned.

That afternoon Sue prayed and she really prayed fervently because she had felt that a Caesarian was out of the question with all of her responsibilities taking care of her

183

soon to be six children, home schooling and a big home. As she prayed, God conveyed to her "Trust in Me and not in your own understanding." He also clearly let her know, "I mean this as a blessing and not as a curse." These were so real to her that she wrote them down and put them in her wallet.

The next day at the hospital, Sue was laboring in the hall and she knew delivery was close. The nurses and technician that she knew were with her. She realized that one push would do it and at that point she told me later, "Mom, God grabbed me by the shoulders and told me not to push!" She told the nurses to call the doctor. He checked her and a foot was out. They took Sue right in the operating room and performed a Caesarian. The cord was wrapped around the neck, an arm was up beside the head and the cord was wrapped around them also. The doctor could hardly dislodge the baby because the cord was so wrapped up that it held the baby tight inside. It was a girl and she is a Down syndrome baby but if God had not been there and directed Sue they may have gone ahead with a normal birth and the baby would have most likely died or at least have cerebral palsy.

Gene and I were at Sue and Marc's home caring for their other five children when Sue called from the recovery room only 20 minutes after the delivery - I don't know how she could be so coherent that soon after surgery but she was. She told me that Miina Catherine (named after Marc's maternal grandmother and Sue's maternal grandmother) was a beautiful girl 6 pounds, 10 ounces, 20" long and had Down syndrome. My heart was filled with love and concern for Sue and I longed to be with her. Though my heart raced for a moment, God gave me a great joy and I knew that Miina was a Gift to us from God. Rachael, Daniel, Anna, Mikaela and Abram were thrilled to have a baby sister. The phone lines worked overtime as we let everyone in the family know about the precious addition to our family. Everyone reacted with great love and compassion: Bruce and Linda were able to go immediately because they both work in Elmira where Sue was in the hospital and Linda continued going during every break that she had because her school was only two blocks away. Tom went as soon as he could leave work in Corning and the rest of us went as soon as we could get there. Many tears

184

were shed but I noticed how bright the eyes were behind the tears and how radiant the faces were. God touched every one of us and when we laid eyes on that precious bundle of love we just melted - she won the hearts of the whole bunch of us for life! Tom's Linda loved her sight unseen and couldn't wait to hold her. Rebecca felt, as I did, that she was a blessing from God and said she would call Mark on his cell phone. He called me soon after and said, "Mom, I am flooded with joy." Tom called me from his cell phone on his way to and from the hospital and the intense love in his voice

Miina with her brother Daniel

brought tears to my eyes. Her cousins all loved her and prayed for her several times each day. Summer expressed her love and concern by being with Sue and calling to offer her help with the children. Miina's brothers and sisters loved her immediately and that love grows by leaps and bounds. They hover over her like flies and keep her motivated which has proven to be beneficial.

Miina was in Neonatal for ten days and on oxygen for three weeks. Down syndrome babies have weak muscles and many have a difficult time nursing but we were fortunate that she was eager to eat (a family characteristic) right from the beginning. We are also pleased

with her progress - her hearing, eyesight and heart are strong and she responds according to her age level in normal babies. Her smiles and baby talk are beautiful. She also started rolling over at an early age so we will see as time goes on how the progress will continue. We are all hopeful. She is unbelievably good, always happy and almost never cries.

Miina spreading her joy

185

Sue's first reaction to the news about Miina was one of confusion but she told me, "It was evident that the hand of God was working so therefore who was I to believe that my illusion of perfection could compare with God's perfect plan?!" Soon after Miina's birth, Marc's back healed. The nurses and technician were aware that something beautiful happened and Sue was able to convey God's loving care to them during her hospital stay and they were visibly moved. God is so wonderful! It is remarkable how Miina has drawn us all even closer. See how she has blessed us already? And we can only be assured that those blessings will be compounded as the years go by.

Thank You God for Your perfect gift of Miina to our family! We love her and her trust in and love for us fills our hearts with joy and thanksgiving. Thank You for blessing our lives!

Sue with five of their six

This little chunk of land where we live is a special haven to us. Knowing that God has placed us here and that He is the real Owner helps us want to be good stewards of what He provides. We love to go away (even if it is only to go to Elmira to buy our weekly groceries) just because we take such pleasure in returning home. The winding, roller coaster roads always bring us back to this place, nestled in the hills, where the air seems sweeter to us and the breeze seems most refreshing, but that is the way it should be - each of us should find the greatest comfort in being where He has planned for us to live.

Our home rambles around in a sprawling adventurous way, and I get a workout just doing the weekly cleaning. Gene and I close parts of it off in the winter but I always look forward to spring when it can all be opened

186

Our home is hard to photograph because it is nestled in the trees.

Back of our home

Front view from up the road

Gene hoisting the flag

again. It looks the nicest at Christmas time. We used to keep all three fireplaces going but now we only use the one in the kitchen and keep it burning from October to April. We have candlelights glowing in forty of our fifty-some windows as a sign of welcome to people passing by. We decorate inside and out with fresh greens, boughs and pine cones, and love the fragrance they add in combination with whatever I'm making in the kitchen to get ready for the season - cookies, breads, fruitcake, wassail, caramel corn, candies, Christmas potpourri, etc. The other time the house looks best is after spring housecleaning. I love to make it sparkle and let the fresh air flow through the house.

Once the days turn warmer the flowerbeds and garden beckon me to rid them of the fall and winter buildup of residue and make them lovely again. At first it looks hopeless and never ending, but gradually we get it all done and by the first of June, things are in fairly good shape.

188

We live on the corner of Hickory Road and Old Post Lane, and our lawn is large and sprawls around, in keeping with our home, with some large areas to mow, but most of

*The work area end of the family gathering place
and the fireplace in the kitchen*

the lawn is broken up with patches of wooded areas, stonewalls, pe-
rennial beds, vegetable and herb gardens, camp fire area,
paths, hills, rocks and berry bushes. The field that once was
our strawberry patch (the story will come later) is now a wild
flower field.

189

One garden plot planted -
three to go

Pathway to the garden

A pleasant break
from garden
planting

190

*Precious
Cargo*

Campfire and garden

Campfire

191

Flower bed asleep

Flower bed awake

Animals find comfort here as well. We enjoy watching the deer and wild turkeys. The bears stay pretty much out of sight, but through the late spring and summer they frequently visit our

bird feeders and break them down. Gene has almost earned a degree in bird feeder repair! The birds are what excite me, and I have made friends with quite a few of them over the years. For three or four years I had a brown thrasher that came to the garden when I whistled for him, and as I sat weeding he would go from row to row with me, perching on a marking stake nearby to converse with me. The chickadees and wrens are always friendly and I have a mourning dove that likes to burrow in the soft warm garden soil in the afternoon to take a nap. She is so used to my presence that she doesn't even fly away when I weed in the row next to her, and sometimes when it seems especially hot, I

193

A cinnamon bear in our garden

take a container of water and put it beside her. My rose-breasted grosbeaks are quite tame also. Three years ago, one took a special liking to me, and learned to come when I called him. I enjoyed his visits when I sat in the lawn to hull strawberries, pit cherries, shell peas, snip beans, cut up cucumbers for pickles or whatever my excuse was for being outside. He was always close telling me his happy story, and I was telling him how pretty he was - perhaps that's why he loved me. When the days turned cold he and his family left, and I was quite sad to think I might not see him again. The following spring on May 8th, I was watching and listening as I went about my kitchen work because that is the day that many of the colorful birds return to our hill. When I heard the call of a rose-breasted grosbeak, I opened the window above my kitchen sink. With hopeful anticipation, I called to the bird saying, "Welcome home, pretty boy!", but I feared it wouldn't be my little buddy from the summer before. To my delight, a beautiful bird flew to a branch near the window and when I said, "Come here, baby", it flew to the screen in front of my face, clung to the wire mesh and talked to me. My heart was so happy that I told him he was a blessing from God, and we were best friends again for that entire summer.

194

Grandaughter's wreath project

Grandma with Abram & Mikaela

What wonderful blessings God gives us! How rich we are to be counted as His children, and to be cared for by Him. Not only does He provide us with our own suitable shelter, surroundings, flowers and feathered friends, but He also packs us firmly with blessings that are far more significant in measure.

195

Excursion with Grandpa

Tree house

196

I am humbled to be the recipient of an internal gift that God gives to women. He has planted deep within us unique feelings, sharpened our instincts and filled our hearts with overflowing joy and everlasting love for our children. He has given us a priceless treasure - the gift of Motherhood.

I like these verses for Mothers:

> Philippians 4: 4-7: Rejoice in the Lord always and again I say rejoice. Let your gentleness be evident to all. The Lord is near. Do not be anxious about anything, but in everything by prayer and petition with thanksgiving, present your requests to God. And the peace of God, which transcends all understanding, will guard your hearts and your minds in Christ Jesus.

And these are the verses I've written in the front of our children's Bibles:

> Philippians 1: 9-11 And this is my prayer: that your love may abound more and more in knowledge and depth of insight, so that you may be able to discern what is best and may be pure and blameless until the day of Christ, filled with the fruit of righteousness that comes through Jesus Christ - to the glory and praise of God.

One morning recently I was sitting at the kitchen table doing some writing when my attention was drawn to the light that I had mistakenly left on in the oven at the other end of the room. I watched as my bread was baking in the oven. The loaves were nicely rounding on top and the pleasant aroma was beginning to fill the kitchen. Was the warmth coming from the oven, the gentle fire in the fireplace or was it coming from a thankful heart?

It was early April but who would have realized it? The ground was covered with a fresh dusting of snow, the wind was blustery and the birds on the tree limbs and at the feeders were finding it difficult to balance themselves. I was happy to be on the inside looking out!

When I looked back in the oven the loaves were turning golden and would soon be ready to take out to cool. The first loaf would be cut for Gene's and my lunch (I'm thankful Gene can be home for lunch)and later the other cooled loaves would be stored in the freezer.

197

As I watched that batch of bread develop from a few ingredients from my pantry, a little kneading and time for rising, I just had to stop and thank God. His perfect plan of creation provided every grain - everything that went into those loaves of bread. It all seemed quite miraculous to me and then I began to think about something really miraculous and I sat there weeping.

I thought back to the time of creation when "He made man in His own image - in the image of God He created him, male and female He created them to be fruitful - when God saw what He made, He said it was very good."

What a perfect plan He had when He made a woman. Not only did He provide a fertile place for a seed to germinate but He made a dwelling place for our baby to live and grow until it has developed enough to come into the world and during that time we have the opportunity to nurture it.

Think what a perfect creator He is - not only does He provide a place for the baby to grow within the mother but He even changes our heart during that nine-month period. We get surges of excited expectancy, new found feelings of hope and joy, the seeds for unconditional love are beginning to grow and Grace is creeping in. It's as if He is giving us a glimpse of His perfect love - perhaps that explains the glow that many expectant mothers have.

If we already know Jesus maybe those feelings come from some special attention we are getting at that time in our life, or if we have never accepted Him, maybe it is just the nearness of Jesus standing at the door of our heart - giving us a golden opportunity. Letting Him in is the only way we can thank God for His priceless gift of motherhood because Jesus said, "The only way to come to the Father is through Me."

As our four children arrived and grew, the Lord gave me a love for each one of them that was unique, separate, equal and uncontained. Even today each of them knows without a doubt that their Mom loves them with all her heart and soul and yet they are free and independent of me because my love for them comes from Christ. He has also given me a beautiful love for each of their spouses - I love them as if they were

my own! Those wonderful pairs of children have added blessing upon blessing to my life in the treasured lives of sixteen grandchildren and two great grandchildren.

When my cup is so full it is hard to express my thanks to God for His gift of motherhood to me, but I can start by accepting this precious gift as I accept His others. To me, the gifts He gives are like ever-blooming flowers on my kitchen table and the sweet fragrances that come from them are the fruits of the Spirit: love, joy, peace, patience, kindness, goodness, faithfulness, gentleness and self control. How rich are His gifts when we love Him and yet - they are free for the asking!

No wonder we say "Rejoice in the Lord always - and again I say rejoice!"

In October 1994 my Mom died and though we were comforted to know that she was relieved of her pain and suffering and could take her place with my Dad in the presence of Jesus, it was difficult for all of us because she had always been an integral part of our lives. The months before she died were filled with concern for her as her health failed and the months afterward were difficult as Gene and I spent the dreary winter sorting through the years of treasures and accumulation in her large home. We prepared for a two-day auction in March 1995. The days were easier after the auctioneer and his wife were there working with us each day. We were ready for spring that year. God is so wonderful to heal our wounds, shed His loving care over us and then give us the added blessing of a fresh new season. As the earth came awake it seems we were able to rise up again also.

It was good news for all of us when Bruce and Linda decided to buy Mom's home. The old homestead had many memories for each of us and we were glad to know it would stay in our family. Bruce and Linda just love it there and have done much to restore it. They have done their part in keeping the whole Wilber clan closely tied to them and the homestead by the times they have invited us there for various reasons but one thing we especially enjoy and look forward to each year is Wreath

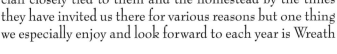

Day the Saturday after Thanksgiving. Bruce, Mat, Cole and Luke build a big bon fire, set up tables nearby for the wreath making and Gene has previously gathered a wagon load of evergreen boughs from our pine and spruce forest, hauled it over and parked it near the tables. Linda and Summer have been busy getting the house ready, making large kettles of soup for our evening meal and keeping the fire in the fireplace stoked with wood. Bruce has everything ready to start grilling hotdogs for lunch when everyone arrives with added food from each family. Linda carries out her CD player to start the Christmas music to get us all in the Spirit. What a wonderful day we have - filled with smiles, hugs, laughter and hearty conversations! As we work on our wreaths, we watch the children play and we roast chestnuts over the coals in the bonfire and drink hot spiced cider when we need refreshment. (The children consume a lot of toasted marshmallows and hot chocolate). From the first warm welcome in the early afternoon to the last quiet conversations in their comfortable home late at night - each moment is a treasure to me - a time when we can all enjoy each other, laugh at the antics of the children, interact with the young people and have all the more reasons to count our blessings. I am so thankful for Bruce and Linda and all they do to cement our family together.

Good times and bad cement us together. The whole family was in prayer for Luke last fall. Summer is such a good Mom! Her devotion to her boys is beautiful to behold (she reminds me very much of Linda, her Mom). Luke was fourteen months old and became extremely ill. His blood count was dangerously low and he was so listless, pale and lethargic that even the doctors were alarmed. It is difficult when you see a precious little boy in that condition to not fear for his life. Summer prayed so hard through her tears and God reassured her even before the results of the tests confirmed that it was a milk allergy. It took Luke a long time to recover but he was surrounded by the love and prayers of us all.

Bruce owns Wilber Auto Sales on Pennsylvania Avenue in Elmira and has been in business in that location for over 20 years. 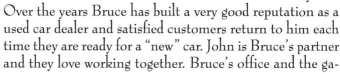 Over the years Bruce has built a very good reputation as a used car dealer and satisfied customers return to him each time they are ready for a "new" car. John is Bruce's partner and they love working together. Bruce's office and the ga-

rage areas are a gathering place for local men who stop in for coffee and casual conversation. Both Bruce and John are very personable and have a real affection for people. Summer walks there each morning adding her uplifting warmth and affection and Cole and Luke think they run the business. Cole has his regular morning chores to do with Bruce and both boys melt the hearts of the men that come. Good natured Joe is able to stop in frequently on his way to or from his work for a trucking firm that contracts out to the postal system. Linda, who is a school nurse at Elmira Free Academy, is compassionately attentive to people's needs. Her sincere concern makes her easy to talk to and her many interests make her fun to be around. She also is able to stop in at the garage one or two times every day. You see - it is a real family operation with each of them contributing their own loving qualities to make Wilber Auto Sales a pleasant place to be.

201

Chapter 24

Grandma

The time before the auction was too short for me to read through the boxes, crates, trunks and baskets of papers, pictures and letters (some dating back to 1812) that I found in Mom's attic; so Gene brought them all to our house and I spent the following winter evenings reading and sorting. Two little treasures that I found were my dear maternal Grandma's diaries. I cannot tell you how it refreshed me to step back in time and read her own sweet thoughts that she wrote so many years before. I knew her well - but now I had been given a new insight.

When Gene and I were married and through the years that followed, our goal was to have a Christ-centered family. After we moved here on our farm and I began working in my garden each year, I began making a comparison between the small cycle of a summer garden and the magnificent cycle of a human life. As we nurture our children with the knowledge of God and a love for Jesus and teach them a little bit here and a little bit there (Isaiah 28:9-10) everyday of their lives about the things of God we will reap a bountiful harvest. We need to realize that we are the greatest influence in our children's lives. Through good times and bad the way we think, the way we act, the way we respond, the way we live will teach them more about behavior than any amount of instruction. Through our example our children can learn patience, kindness and integrity. That can put a heavy load on the parent but we can take heart because Jesus is there to help us every step of the way.

When I read Grandma's diaries it was as if I could see the completed cycle of a Christian life. I clearly saw how enduring and encompassing a well-lived Christian life can be and I realized how much her life had influenced mine.

202

Grandma made everything special just by her presence. She has always from the very beginning, been a part of my life. She read to me, played with me, held me in her arms, told me stories and sang so off key that it was uniquely beautiful. She was very witty and had a wonderful sense of humor so we did a lot of laughing together but if I was upset her concern and love were like healing balm. As I grew up she was my only baby sitter. We made a yo-yo quilt, crocheted potholders and edgings on hankies and did embroidery. We put puzzles together, picked berries and flowers and watched her huge goldfish in her rock garden pond. We went to the corner grocery store to buy groceries so we could cook our favorite food for just the two of us to eat.

When I was seven my Grandpa Ayers (my paternal grandfather) bought me a white fur coat, hat and muff for Christmas. He had more money than Grandma. Some grandmothers get jealous if they can't be the one to give the big gift - but not Grandma. She was so excited that she made a big plan for the two of us to go shopping - all decked out in our fur coats. When the eventful day came for us to have our special outing she helped me into my coat, placed the hat "just so" on my head, and made sure my muff was held properly. Then she put on her black hat (using a lovely hat pin to hold the hat secure) her black kid gloves and her big black fur coat which must have been 15 or 20 years old. But I thought she was the most beautiful woman in Elmira, NY.

We walked one block up Irvine Place (near Elmira College) to the street car and then we rode downtown in style. We both sat so tall I thought I could feel my neck stretching and I would undoubtedly be an inch taller by the end of the day. What fun we had. It seemed to me that everyone knew my Grandma so we got lots of compliments about our fur coats. It was a grand day.

The Junior High School I attended on Washington Avenue was only one block from Grandma's home so I went there every day for lunch. Whenever I sang or played my harp in church or whatever school or college program I was participating in Grandma was there. My friends loved her, so after I got my driver's license I took my friends to visit her. We loved to put puzzles together in the winter and go fishing in the spring. In the summer we would sit on the porch to visit and on special occasions we would sit on the porch steps where we could eat watermelon and spit the seeds on the lawn. (Watermelon was one of her favorite foods.)

Grandma was 79 when Gene and I were married. For many years family members had been doing her shopping for her but our wedding was so special to her that she made the long walk up Irvine Place on a cold December day and took the bus downtown and bought a gift for us - all by herself. Is it any wonder I loved her?! And is it any wonder that I consider the two little diaries Grandma wrote back in 1888 and 1889 when she was 14 and 15, treasures?

The Van B. Smith family lived on a farm near Otego, NY - west of Oneonta. There was Pappa (John Van Buren Smith - related to President Martin Van Buren), Mamma (Diadamia [Damie] Baldwin Smith) and four children - Bertie, Adelaide (my Grandma), Lottie and Erwin.

At the time these diaries were written Erwin had not been born yet and the year before when Grandma was 13 her 16-year old brother, Bertie, was very sick with the mumps. During the night he came to her room and stretched out across the bottom of her bed. He told her he didn't feel well so she turned one of her covers down and spread it over him, rubbed his forehead and patted his back until he went to sleep. Then she lay back down and fell asleep. When she woke up in the morning Bertie was dead at her feet.

They were a close-knit family. My Grandma's Grandma (Hannah Van Buren Smith) lived next door and spent much of her time with them and sometimes the girls went over to her house for dinner. Aunts and Uncles came to visit frequently and visits from cousins were anticipated with joy.

(My Great, great Grandmother Hannah was widowed just two years before these diaries were written. Her husband was John Smith [1812-1886]. He was a school teacher and felt the calling into the ministry when he was eighteen. He was baptized on December 25, 1830 in the Susquehanna River.

204

It was believed that "the ice cold of the river was much less to bear than Hellfire." He became a Baptist minister and was ordained in the Summit, NY church on June 12, 1833. In over fifty years of preaching he worked in an area of 160 square miles where Delaware, Otsego and Schoharie Counties meet. His average salary was about $300 per year and according to his records he baptized 523, married 299 couples and had funerals for 478. He preached about slavery even when abolition was a forbidden topic to be discussed in some public buildings in New York State. He was asked to return for second pastorates in both Oneonta and Summit and helped in the rebuilding of the Summit Church in 1878 at a cost of $2500. At a Baptist Association meeting in Franklin, NY in 1887 it was said of him, "One more standard bearer has fallen, one more watchman's voice is hushed. Let us be admonished to gird on the armor and move on to certain victory.")

Winters were harsh, springs were refreshing and summers were busy. They had quite a large farm not far from the Susquehanna River and planted fields of oats, millet and potatoes. Grandma milked six to ten cows morning and night and took the milk to the "factory" in the evening with horse and wagon - sometimes Aunt Lottie would ride with her. During hay season Grandma did the raking (with a horse) and helped get the hay in the barn. She ironed, helped clean house, baked pies on baking day, practiced piano at least an hour a day and never complained.

Every Sunday they attended church morning and evening. Grandma always wrote the name of the minister and the text he used for his sermon. While they were visiting her Mamma's parents in Elmira on Sunday, September 8, 1889, she went to hear Thomas K. Beecher preach in the morning with her parents and then in the evening she went back to hear him again with her Grandma.

The school year was not at all like we have now. They went from April 30 to July 20 and then from October 22 to March 16. The one room school house had eight grades but only six scholars (as Grandma called them) and many days there were only three in attendance - Grandma, Aunt Lottie and their friend Hattie.

205

I would like you to read some of Grandma's entries. Her vernacular is very typical of that time period and I love it. Notice the difference in the way she wrote Bible chapters and verses. I am omitting the little weather report she gave at the beginning of each entry.

Sunday, Jan. 1, 1888
Welcome - Went to church today the text was Luke 13 chapter and 6-9 verses. The minister is staying here now. Went to church at night the text was Exodus 8 chapter 10 verse. Grandma has got the headache.

Monday Jan. 2
I began me a pair of stockings today. I went a skating. Pappa rode the pony to the village today - he got me a bottle of cologne. The snow has gone off. It is very icy.

Thursday Jan. 26
We are at Aunt Ann's - the road was drifted so Ma, Lottie and I had to walk. We are not a going on to New Milford. It was very cold and windy this forenoon but it is a little pleasanter this afternoon.

Friday Jan. 27
Am at Unadilla yet. We were going on but it stormed. I want to live more for Jesus in the future. We have played dominoes all the evening.

Saturday Jan. 28
We started from Uncle Myrt's this morning. Stopped at Afton and took dinner and went on to about 5 miles of Susquehanna and got stuck in a snow drift and had to stay all night. Lottie and I stayed to a Mrs. Terrell's.

Sunday Jan. 29
Did not go to church. Went over to a Mr. Roger's and spent the day. The men shuffled out the road.

Monday Jan. 30
Reached New Milford all safe and sound.

Wednesday Feb. 8

We have got home all safe and sound. The water froze up. It was colder - the wind blew and it snowed. We had to went in the lots three times coming from Unadilla - the drifts were very deep.

Wednesday Feb. 15

It has been very windy and unpleasant. I want to be a better Christian. Mamma is 42 years old today.

Feb. 24

I have been working on the crazy quilt.

Mar. 3

Pappa gave me an orange today.

Mar. 12

A foot of snow fell.

Mar. 13

Two feet of snow on the ground.

Mar. 17

It has been a pleasant day. Today Pappa went to the Village and then to Wells Bridge and got a puppy. I want to do some good in the world and be some use to my God.

Mar. 19

Pappa sold the puppy.

Mar. 26

Pappa gave me an image in the form of a little girl. It has been warmer. Mamma washed.

Mar. 29

It snowed in the night but is pleasant now. Pappa tapped the sap bush. We pasted pictures.

Apr. 6

It has been quite pleasant. We went up to Mrs. Randall's today. I began me a necktie quilt. We sugared off.

207

Apr. 7

It has been pleasant. I have got 47 blocks done toward my quilt. Pappa got some oranges today - he got some calico to set my quilt together with.

Apr. 9

I have tried to be good today. I do want to be good.

Apr. 13

I got my blocks all done for my quilt today and Mamma finished setting it together.

Apr. 14

It has been quite rainy. Lottie went over to Mrs. Knapp's. I went to Mrs. Randall's - she gave me a lot of calicoes for my crazy quilt.

Apr. 30

School commenced today. Pappa has sown with oats one piece.

June 18

I do want to be more like Jesus.

June 19

We all went over to the Village. We recited our pieces. I have got a crow named Jim - his leg and wing is broke. Oh! He is very nice. I bathed him today.

June 23

Lottie and I went a strawberrying - got enough for a shortcake.

June 24

It was children's day at the M.E. and Baptist church. I went and spoke. I went to church this evening.

June 29

Society was held here today. There was 36 here and they got $3.83.

July 3

Mary, Lottie and I were the only ones in school today. I have got a hen come off with 21 little chicks. Lottie went to the factory with Pappa - he got some firecrackers.

July 4

They quilted today. There was no school today. Lottie and I went up to Mrs. Randalls with some patterns for her to stamp and in the evening to see the fireworks - they were very nice - got home at 9:45.

July 7

It has been very pleasant. I went a strawberrying and then raked. Mamma is reading a good sermon. She has just read a good book. It says we are writing a book to be read at eternity. Oh! I want to be more like our blessed Lord.

July 8

It has been pleasant. We all went to church - herd a sermon by Elder Sheppard. His text was John Chapter 1 and 2-3 verses. When we read of the noble lives of Christians it made me feel as if it was grand to be good and I do want to be good.

Jan 1. 1889

I want to live nearer to Christ this year than I did last.

I could go on and on. I got so lost in her early life that I laughed and cried. I found myself being extra thankful for my washer, running hot water, our car, our tractor and all the work-saving things that we have today - and yet I have been left with a yearning for my grandchildren, great grandchildren and all children to be able to grow up in such an innocent way. We can not step back in time but we *can* focus on the good, the pure, the lovely and the Godly in our homes.

When Grandma was 18 she was the teacher in that little country school that she wrote about in her diary. A few years later the family left the farm and moved to Elmira where they had purchased a new home on Davis Street just one block from Elmira College. This gave Grandma the opportunity to start college when she was 21 and she graduated in the class of 1899 when she was 25.

209

Grandma

That year she moved from home to take a teaching position. Since her lifelong habit was to attend church she went to the Methodist Church the very first Sunday after she arrived in town and was pleased to find a very fine minister there. It turned out that he was a widower. He was highly respected. As Grandma became involved in the community it seemed

quite natural for them to get acquainted but she hadn't imagined they would fall in love (he was her first love). They were married when Grandma was 29.

They had five little girls - Marguerite, Ruth, Catherine (my Mom) Laura and Doris (who died when she was just a few days old). Soon after that Grandpa got sick and died when my Mom was only five years old. While he was ill Grandma attended Lima Theological Seminary so she could carry on his duties.

After Grandpa's death Grandma moved her family back to Elmira to live the rest of her life in the family home on Davis Street. Because her Pappa and Mamma were there to help with the girls she was able to teach Biology at Elmira Free Academy and on Sundays she taught a ladies Sunday School class at Hedding Methodist Church. That was in 1913 and I remember visiting her Sunday School class in the 1940's where she was still teaching - those ladies had such a joyful bond.

As I grew older (18-25) I began to notice tears in Grandma's eyes when I dropped in to surprise her. She sat in her chair next to the bay window where she could look out and see her pink rambling rose bush that had climbed up and hung heavily over the white arbor that arched above the walkway that went along the side of her house. Her well-worn Bible was in her aproned lap or on the lamp table beside her. I never could tell if the tears were shed while she prayed for her family or if she just felt especially close to the Lord and her thankful heart was spilling out of her eyes - as mine does.

The last time I saw her was in September 1955. Bruce was 21 months old and Thomas was 2-1/2 months old. She called them "her boys" and held them or played with them to her heart's content. I was so glad we made that trip home from Kingsville, Texas because she died of cancer three months later. I am sure you can imagine how deeply grieved I was. I would miss her terribly but at the same time the Lord gave me a blessed peace because I knew, without a doubt, that she was with Jesus whom she had loved and served so faithfully since she was a little girl.

Revelation 21:4 says "And God will wipe away every tear from their eyes...." Grandma will never shed another tear or feel another pain or worry about the money for next week's groceries or use the same tea bag for a week. God gives eternal joy to those who love Him. Heaven is far too wonderful to even imagine.

Grandma's life leads me toward heaven where I know she is saving a place for me. It has made me want to make sure that all my family will go there. Years ago I began to realize that I wanted to meet my old friends and neighbors, my choir members, the Bible Study ladies, my Quilt Shop employees and friends and many others that Jesus has been putting me in touch with. I wanted to meet them all in heaven so I have been praying that any who might not already know Christ personally will give their life to Him. Most of the people I am around now seem to be getting younger and according to the law of averages - I will probably get to heaven first and when I do I will be saving a place!

Grandma never knew or assumed that the cycle of her life could make a difference in my life or anyone else's and yet - here 128 years after she was born I am telling everyone what an impact she made on my life. None of us stop to think about the way we affect others or how powerful our influence can be but I hope this makes us stop to think about it. We want to gently lead our families to Christ. It won't happen if we push and shove but - as we live for Christ they will be drawn to Him.

Grandma's humble openness to Christ gave Him the freedom to work through her life. She had a high calling - to live to glorify Christ. We have that same calling. We can open the hearts of others by glorifying Him in everything that we do - for this generation and generations to come.

212

213

Chapter 25

The Patchwork of My Life

Before Gene left for Vietnam in early April 1968, I put all my needle work and art supplies away and laughingly told him that he was my inspiration and I would get them out again when he returned. He always encouraged me to be creative and I appreciated his wood working abilities. We also enjoyed refinishing antiques together. When I made that statement to him I never realized he would be gone for five years and by 1970 I was beginning to feel a strong need for a creative outlet.

The days were crammed with work, activity and responsibility from the time I got up for prayer and devotions until the children went to bed - but then the late evening hours before I went to bed were not as easy. While I was sitting on the sofa one night my attention was drawn to the antique quilt that was decoratively placed at the opposite end of the sofa. I pulled it onto my lap and began studying it to see how it was constructed. As I gently pulled at the seams to see how the piecing was done the Lord put a love in my heart for the woman that had made it. Then I had to go around the house and gather together more old quilts and pile them around me on the sofa.

The utilitarian quilt had bigger stitches and I could almost see the gnarled, hard-working hands of a farm woman who lovingly provided the covers to keep her family warm. I discovered the worn binding at the top of the quilt and realized that this had been on Mamma and Pappa's bed - his rough whiskers had caused the fabric to wear thin. In contrast I visualized the adept fingers of the woman who made an intricately appliquéd quilt. Her precise and uniform stitches produced an heirloom masterpiece. I experienced the love that a young woman

felt as she made a cradle sized quilt for the baby she was expecting. Each quilt that I studied gave me a refreshing insight of the person that made it and the Lord began filling my own thoughts with the desire to make a quilt.

Since there was no one around to teach me - I decided to make a simple nine-patch but I wanted my center square - the very first block I ever made, to be special. I appliquéd a red calico heart on a 12" muslin square and then embroidered this pledge around the heart - "Each stitch will be done in love to bind me still closer to my family, my friends and God up above."

Oh - how could I imagine the significance of that small beginning in my life? As I stitched (by hand) and thought and prayed - excitement was welling within me! I loved putting the colors together and I'd hurry to finish a few blocks and press them before I went to bed so I could show the children in the morning. "Simple pleasures" some may say - but to me - something to anticipate and enjoy during the lonely winter evenings. Piece by piece and block by block the quilt grew into a bedspread size quilt top and then it was put away as warmer weather arrived.

Because Gene came home in 1973 the quilt top remained in a blanket chest until the winter of 1976 when Gene was recuperating from his thyroid operation. I had the quilt on a frame in the dining room and he was generally sitting by the fire at the kitchen fireplace. It was difficult to visit in shouting voices so I asked him to sit by me at the quilt frame. Gradually he started threading my needles and soon after that he was quilting with me. All of the children and Mom quilted on that quilt. We enjoyed it and found it to be a real gathering place!

Because of my age - I have a wonderful advantage! I can look back over my life and liken it to a patchwork quilt. The fabrics that make up the center are a bright and cheery collage, dancing with daisies, dandelions, violets, pussy willows, buttercups, Christmas presents, Easter baskets, dolls and pets. The threads that hold it together are strong family ties and the whole random effect depicts the carefree abandon of a happy childhood.

215

Some quilts carry on with carefree abandon but mine has a radiant material that frames the center section of the quilt. If you look closely you will see that the quilting thread is pure spun gold and miraculously it is continuous - unbroken. The stitches are perfect and very intricate. The framing is only an inch wide but it is the focal point of the whole quilt. It represents Jesus - when He called a thirteen-year-old girl and she opened her heart and asked Him to come in.

The patchwork blocks that surround the framing are interesting to look at now - my mature eye can see how imperfect the points are and how some of the pieces are quite askew. The prayers that were being said then were as typical as any happy young teenager, but those blocks are as strongly attached to the radiant framing as the next blocks which represent a time when the prayers became more heartfelt - a time of awareness when my thanksgiving for and joy because of His loving Presence drew me to tears. I wanted to do His will, to serve Him and to be used by Him.

Christ became the primary color in each block of my quilt and I began praying for the unknown husband and children I would have. In due time, as they came into my life, they became the other coordinating primary fabrics. They were the perfect match because they were chosen by God to be a part of my life.

I regret the times that I was a little headstrong and added pieces that were soiled and damaged but even then - His forgiveness cleansed them and made them whole.

Anyone can tell that God was the great designer of my quilt because He included scraps that I never would have used! If it had been left up to me - only the things I enjoyed would be a part of my life - my quilt. But now I recall - I have always asked Him to use me and He uses us best through our weaknesses.

One of the weaknesses from my life that I would have thrown in the scrap bag is book reports! When I was in school we had to walk up to the front of the class to give our book reports - my knees knocked and I almost got sick to my stomach. It was bad enough when in elementary school we had to stand beside our desk to read aloud (at least the desk would break

216

my fall if I should faint) - But walking up and standing before that class drained the color from my face and I still recall the fever like flush that came over me after the report was completed and I had returned to my seat.

Oh, surely - if I could discard something and never do it again it would be standing in front of a group of people to talk. But God has put me there and the verse that rings in my mind again is II Corinthians 12:9 "My grace is sufficient - my power is perfected in your weakness." Now I can talk to people joyfully because Christ is in my heart, working through my weakness and I do it to glorify God.

Music has always been an important part of my life. When I was a music major at Mansfield I loved all the subjects except directing - it rated almost equal to book reports. I decided to work hard to get a good grade - but I knew directing was going to be my scrap to get rid of. Wouldn't you know that God chose directing to be the one continuous thread to be sewn into my life?! I have directed choirs for over fifty years with His help. How I love it! It is done only to praise and bring glory to Him!

You can easily see how the Primary color shines throughout my quilt. Some blocks have more Highlights than others - they were the times I had to lean on Him more or even be lifted over the rough areas. But the part of the quilt that was made during the five years Gene was a POW almost sparkles! Many people expect that to be the dark and gloomy part of my quilt where blacks and grays were used and tear stains damaged the fabric and they seem quite surprised to see that it nearly glows. There are areas of Trapunto (a design that is outlined with a quilting stitch and then stuffed with batting or cotton from beneath to raise and empha- size the pattern). Those sections represent the extra padding I got from the Holy Spirit - my Comforter. He was my intercessor that first night when it was too hard to pray and then He provided all the fruit I needed to sustain me. With all the help I received from the Three in One - God the Father, Jesus Christ the Son and the Holy Spirit - how could I call the experience any- thing but a blessing and count it for joy?!

217

One evening in late spring of 1981 I was weeding in our garden and Gene was getting ready for a school board meeting. He came out to say goodbye but stopped to talk to me about a concern he had about the dedication of a teacher. He left with his last thought ringing in my ear. Now that our children were grown he wondered if I would consider teaching again - he knew how I loved children and how much I had enjoyed being a music teacher 31 years earlier - before we were married.

My garden is one of my favorite places to talk to Jesus and oh! how I talked to Him that night! I sensed a change coming in my comfortable life. I realized that Gene worked hard as a commuter pilot and that expenses were greater with children in college and that I should be helping to carry the load - but teach again? I had forgotten so much! I realized I would have to go back to school.

Each avenue of thought disturbed me more and as I prayed about it I told the Lord I just wanted to serve Him and please Gene. I also added "But please - if there is something You would have me do here at home I would be grateful." I wanted to be available for Gene, our four children, the addition of two wives and three grandchildren to the family and my Mom.

Within a week Sue and Linda (Tom's wife) were thinking about summer work. We thought of a cottage industry making and selling patchwork items. Tom organized everything, made up a brochure and advertised in Early American Life and Yankee magazines. Orders started arriving by the end of June but by then both girls had summer jobs. We were all busy but I remember working late at night to complete orders. I prayed for the woman and tucked a little potpourri under the tissue paper when I wrapped each item.

By late August the garden needed constant care and fall meetings would be starting soon. When Tom and Linda came for dinner after church I talked to Tom about putting an end to the cottage industry. He planned to send notices to all of our customers. I mentioned that it would have been a lot more fun to have sold the fabric from the bolt - then I would be able to see, talk to and get acquainted with each woman.

The next Sunday while the family was enjoying dinner Tom told me that he had put ads in the local Pennysavers so I could sell the 15 bolts of fabric we had. I started pouring out the reasons I couldn't do that, "I don't know how to measure 5/8 yard of fabric" - "I don't know how to calculate the tax" - "Why I have never even worked in a store!"

Finally Gene spoke up from the other end of the table. He told me to settle down and then he said "Who on earth would drive way out here to buy fabric anyway?!"

That did it! I was suddenly excitedly challenged. I would drive that far ...and then I started praying and planning for the opening of my tiny dining room shop in three days.

Sunday was busy with the family. Monday my friend, Gloria (our Pastor's wife), and I taught two tole painting classes and I canned tomatoes when I got home. Tuesday morning I cleaned house and worked on the Bible Study lesson for the class that I taught in our home each Tuesday afternoon. Tuesday evening I had an educational organization meeting in Mansfield while Gene went to a School Board meeting in Troy. When we returned home at 10:30 PM we turned our dining room into an inviting little quilt shop. The table was my counter with a yardstick taped to the table pad - the right side of the pad would be my cutting guide to get a nice straight edge. An antique box was my money box and beside it was a guide that Tom had made for me. He calculated all the fractions I would need to use (I had never even used a calculator!). The 15 bolts of fabric were arranged in stacks that coordinated on a deacons' bench and hired man's bed. The few notions, eyelet trim and pillow forms that we had were placed around in a variety of baskets. When I turned off the light I said a prayer.

Early the next morning I cut letters out of fabric and glued them on a board. That first sign only said "Calico Shop" but it looked like a cheery welcome when I placed it on a bench on the front porch. (The official name would be "The Strawberry Patch Calico Shop" but I didn't have a board that long.)

Perhaps this Strawberry Patch Calico Shop would turn out better than our experience with a strawberry patch

1-1/2 years earlier. Through all the years we had enjoyed picking our year's supply of strawberries. We loved every phase of it, from the family outing in the field to the eating of the succulent fresh fruit. Our memories of sitting together in the lawn hulling berries are sweet, and preserving them is easy. We never knew which way we liked them best - fresh, in shortcake or pie, topping vanilla ice cream or cereal, made into jam and spread on warm homemade bread, or just sliced in a bowl with sugar and milk. Since we had such a passion for strawberries it seemed appropriate for us to use part of our own land to grow them. In the spring of 1980, we prepared a portion of the field beyond our garden and lawn for our strawberry patch. Gene plowed and dragged, we all picked stones and discarded clumps of sod with quack grass, we added compost and kept working the soil until it was soft and ready for the 800 plants that we meticulously planted in nice straight rows. After the planting was done, we made several trips with the little tractor and trailer up to our pines, where we raked pine needles and loaded them into the trailer and took them back to neatly mulch around our tiny plants. The Spring rain made them grow profusely and soon they blossomed and then the blossoms turned into fruit. Strawberries should not be picked the first year in order that the plants will grow stronger and establish themselves. So we looked longingly at our first berries but went to a commercial field to pick again that year.

Summer came and the rains stopped. We had no water supply in the field so had to start carrying 27 pails of water to the plants each day. Drought conditions continued throughout that whole summer and we faithfully carried water to our thirsty plants. Strawberry plants produce runners and we snipped off all but the four strongest ones from each plant. We had allowed space for these added babies when we planted the original 800 mother plants. As these strong runners produced rooting plants, we gently guided them to the loose soil in the row so they could secure their roots in their permanent home, and we watered them carefully. In the fall, we mulched them again with pine needles to help them survive our harsh winter.

I couldn't wait for the warm days of spring to see how our plants had fared through the cold winter. What a joy to pull the mulch aside and see 3200 perky strawberry plants hungry for sunshine and rain which God provided very beautifully that spring. We worked with them eagerly as we anticipated our first crop. In early June, I went out to pull weeds one morning and loosen the pine needles in the rows. The plants were a picture - vibrant green leaves and large white blossoms with a touch of yellow in the centers. Some berries were beginning to form, and that was an exciting sight to behold.

When I went back to the house, Mom called and asked me to come over for a few minutes, so I jumped in the truck and drove over to her house to help her with a little project. Within 30 minutes, I was on my way back home and couldn't wait to crane my neck and see how the strawberry patch looked from the road. I noticed a tractor in our upper field as I came over the hill. He was plowing to prepare the land for planting. Just beyond the hedge row of maples that arch over the road, I looked to catch my first glimpse of our strawberry patch, and my heart sank to the pit of my stomach. Our whole field had been plowed - the strawberry plants had disappeared below the surface, and fresh furrows of earth were on top of them.

I hurriedly parked the truck and ran to the strawberry patch. On my knees I dug elbow deep through the soil, but it was of no use - the plants were ruined. What a sorry sight I was -helplessly kneeling there in the moist earth wiping tears away with the backs of my soil-covered hands, leaving muddy smudges on both cheeks. Sometimes we toil and work for nothing, but through it all we are learning and growing. You may wonder about our reaction to the farmer - no ill feelings at all - he was a life-long friend, and loving friends are far more important than a few hundred plants. He was there plowing our field for his son to use, and he had no idea that we had planted strawberries in the section of the field that we had retained for our own use. Besides, God was about to give me a Strawberry Patch that I could more easily take care of for Him, and hopefully the Patch would bear fruit that would be more pleasing to Him than strawberries!

On that September morning when the Strawberry Patch Calico Shop opened, I prayed again that Jesus would use me to serve anyone that came. I prayed that He would

221

give me a special love for them and that His Peace would fill our home. At 9:00 two women arrived and soon another and then another. How we enjoyed each other! I was thankful to have instant hot water in the kitchen. It made it easy to serve spiced tea.

There was a gentle flow of customers that week and even though we did not advertise the next week - the flow continued - we never had a day without a customer. I started teaching pillow classes around the kitchen table (my dear friends in my Bible Study made up the first class) and by January I was so busy in the shop that I had to invite a teacher in to start quilt classes. The dining room was full and benches of fabric lined the hallway so we started carpeting the loft - we were thankful it had an outside entrance. It made a lovely shop and we moved there the next July.

From then on the business flourished. I sent out two class letters a year and we filled 75 to 85 classes each spring and fall. We carpeted and stenciled Gene's garage and used that as a classroom with overflow in the kitchen and dining room. The women loved it and we thoroughly enjoyed them!

Crafters came to buy their fabric and stuffing from us and when they did shows they told others about our shop. I appreciated all the extra customers they brought to the shop so I decided to repay them. On the third Saturday in October 1982, I invited eight of them to set up in the lower end of our shop. We took the fabric out of that end to give them enough space and added a few benches in the upper end to accommodate the overflow fabric. I even put neat stacks of fabric on my counter because I didn't plan to do any business that day. I had advertised for them and it was their day. Cars started filling our parking lot at 8:00 AM and then they were parking along the road as far as we could see. When we opened the door at 9:00 it was unbelievable. God even sent beautiful crowds - they were orderly, warm, friendly, polite and eager. They loved the crafts and after the customers bought from the crafters they wanted to buy fabric so we emptied the counter and started cutting. What a joyous busy day! The crafters each said it was their best show ever. The following year we had food, outside exhibitors and vendors in the garage. Each year it grew until we had vendors in four large tents, indi-

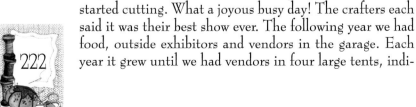

222

Our new shop

vidual canopies on four lawns, a loft full and a garage full, Greek and American food and heritage crafters and Gene had two fields ready for parking. I kept my original purpose and never charged the vendors for their space here.

We outgrew our loft so Gene built a post and beam carriage shed type building right across the dirt road from our home. It was exciting to see it go up and as the completion time drew near I wondered how we were going to move all that inventory. Gene, Sue and I were strong but that would be a lot of trips! I was also concerned because many of our customers were out of advertising range. People came from Southern PA, New Jersey, and all over New York State, Canada and New England. Imagine how anyone would feel to drive that distance and find us unable to take care of them. My prayers were answered. One day two customers offered to help and then some more and by the time moving Monday came we had such a crowd of helpers that the line started at the top step in the loft, went down the stairs, through the hallway, out the door, down the sidewalk, over the driveway, across the road, along the shop drive, up the step, over the deck and into the new building where we had tables set up for each color. I called it the Calico Brigade - no one in line had to move their feet - they just passed the fabric from one person to the next. Two Strawberry Patch teachers were in the loft so they had

223

to move to keep the flow going and Gene, Sue and I were in the shop to take care of everything as it came in. It was a beautiful April day and we had plenty of food for everyone's lunch. We all made a circle, held hands and prayed before we ate. Gene, Sue and I worked long into that night and got everything arranged for business to start again the following morning.

At first Evie from my Bible Study helped me and then my friend Jan helped and she continued to give her faithful help and support throughout the years. Sue started working after that and when we moved it was evident I had to hire a full-time employee. It took much prayer and I was delighted when the answer to my prayer turned out to be Nancy. I had known her all her life and she was a flower girl in our wedding. Not only was Nancy a wonderful Christian but she also was a trusted friend. The shop was well used each day by the customers and it had always been my practice to keep it very clean and have every bolt neatly stacked in its place when the shop opened at 9:00 AM. Nancy kept the shop the same way and I was pleased. One summer I enjoyed having Holly, the daughter of dear friends of ours from church work with me. As time went by I began to pray for another girl to hire and Jo Ann is the one He sent me. Jo Ann was one of those special people that you want to hug. She had been a customer and we already had a sweet relationship. Jo Ann and Nancy had never met but God made them best friends just by putting them together. The next time I prayed for help Flora came to work for me - she was another customer who had become a friend and teacher. Flora was very competent, efficient and knowledgeable. Then one last time I had to hire one more girl and the Lord brought me Karen. She was creative, wonderful and had such a pleasant personality! These girls were treasures to me. We could be concerned together, we could be downright silly, we could get all choked up and cry together, we could just about do anything together and be in tune with each other because...we could pray together. How I love those girls!

Gene and I started doing shows the first year I was in business. We started by going to the Troy Fair on quilt day. We took standing racks for fabric, trays of Quilters Quarters and precut half-yards. We also took a few baskets of notions, a

224

Our booth at a Natural Quilt Show

crate of books and decorated the booth with quilts and handcrafted gift items. Next we were invited to Guild Shows, big seminars and National shows. Gene had to quit flying because my business had mushroomed and sometimes we were gone 150 days a year doing shows. We had a truck and van trailer to carry our show inventory of 500+ bolts and we had 6,000+ in the shop.

We had many behind the scenes workers and volunteers. The first quilts I sold were made by Susie - a dear Mennonite friend, and then I started selecting the patterns and color combinations. Bernice did the piecing for a short time and then my close friend Kathy, did the piecing and appliqué for the remaining years. Shirley, Marge, Arlene, Judy, Helen, Miriam or Carol did most of the quilting and Mary or Kathy did the tied quilts and Jan always contributed when I needed her. There were about 175 crafters who worked at home and brought their creations to the shop. We did a mail order business and shipped fabric not only all over the United States and Canada but also to Australia, Germany, Norway, Isle of Jersey, Japan, etc. Many guilds came by the busload. If they came in the winter they ate at our classroom tables and in the summertime we always had picnic tables set up for anyone who wanted to bring their lunch. Many times the customers took a break by going for a long walk up the dirt road and through our woodlands. By this time we had 250 acres. We had customers come on horseback, cross-country skis, snowmobiles and motorcycles.

For 15 years the Lord used me to serve Him through "The Strawberry Patch." It never surprised me when He moved everyone away from the counter except a woman who needed to share a problem or he put me on the deck opening UPS shipments when another woman had a heavy heart and we could sit on the step and visit. Every night I had women or families to pray for and every morning I prayed for His blessing on the people that were coming that day. Countless women walked in and said, "I think I've died and gone to heaven!" As I smiled and welcomed them - my heart was saying, "Thank You, God!" Many people - even with the din of laughter, chatter and music from our Christian radio station, Family Life Network, came to me and remarked about the Peace that they felt while they were there - again my heart sang, "Thank You, Lord!"

How can I ever thank Him enough for answering my garden prayer that spring evening in 1981 in such a beautiful way? To think He could use even me - with no experience or knowledge of business. The glory is His but the rewards of love and concern for thousands of women I would have never met has enriched me and the strengthening of my faith to trust Him completely has blessed my life beyond measure.

My life since "The Strawberry Patch" has been rich and full. Time spent with our four families are moments treasured for me and when they are all here I watch them interact with each other and I am tearfully thankful (my children notice and give me an extra hug to help subside the flow but the hugs only bring on more overflowing joy). I spent three and one-half years as a Titus woman for a MOPS (Mothers of Pre Schoolers) group and had the great pleasure of getting well acquainted with a caring group of young mothers. As their Spiritual leader (Titus 2:3-5) I spent much time with them and talked to them mostly about their own relationship with Jesus (the wellspring of our joy) and the advantages of having a Christ-centered marriage, family and home. I had fun encouraging them to love the things I love and taught them the joy of keeping an orderly home, enjoying their children and loving this time in their lives. Our church is family - from Ken and Gloria (pastor and his wife) to the people in our Sunday School class, to the friends throughout the congregation, to the young people and children. Then there are the Cantata singers and Catherine (the piano player, regular choir director and dear friend) - I can't even think of all their beautiful faces and the sweet faces of those in the Children's Choir without having the floodgates open again. These are the people we have been with for twenty-two years - our children grew up together (and now we have their children to love and look after), we have picnicked, picked blueberries, worked at the church, shared everything from burdens to favorite recipes, worshiped and prayed together. We are best friends. We have a huge wooden cross at the front of our church that Ken made (he has built most of a large addition on our church with a little help from a few members). That cross strengthens us each week as we are reminded of what Jesus did for us on the cross and through His resurrection. It is a meaningful reminder to

227

Our Church

me of God's grace. When I realize my own unworthiness to God's favor and the great sacrifice He made when He sent His Son to die on the cross in order for our sins to be forgiven, I am overwhelmed. We can't find real joy in our own circumstances but when we accept this truth and respond to Jesus we will find that we can truly rejoice in Him - in His goodness - in His grace and mercy - in His forgiveness - in His faithfulness. This is the secret of rejoicing and the reason for a heart that overflows with thanksgiving!

We each are in the process of living a life that can be mediocre or glorious - one that barely gets by or one that soars. God gave us the ability to choose. I think now you know the secret of choosing the joy filled life (Read Romans 8). Sometimes you think you cannot go on because of some disaster that is happening in your life but think again and take time to ask for His help - you will be surprised at how lovingly He will work things out for you.

Perhaps my imagination is stimulated because of the stories I make up to tell my grandchildren, but I think about silly things, sometimes about being a stone. I would rather be a small stone in the bottom of a creek than a rock in the bottom of a stagnant pond. The rock gets all muddy and

228

slimy and sluggish as it wallows there in the boggy ooze, but the stone in the creek gets washed and scrubbed and polished by the constant flow of living water. Its life isn't always sunshine and dewdrops - sometimes the muddy, turbulent flood waters beat hard and relentlessly against it and try to suction it from its bed, but the hard times always subside and the gentle refreshing babble returns and the sunlight filters through again to warm it and show that it has become smoother and more brilliant. God plans things that way - He isn't responsible for all the bad tings that happen in life - He has a strong adversary here in this world who leads people astray but God is more than conqueror. We need to put on His breast-plate and shield (Ephesians 6:11) to overcome that evil one and allow him no room in our hearts. God will always still the waters of our turmoil. We must continue to pray and grow in Him and lean not on our own understanding, just give it all to Him and He will raise us up to soar above or in spite of the problem and make us sparkle because of the polishing we have had. God works in unex-pected ways throughout each of our lives. Whenever you feel over-whelmed, discouraged or anxious, turn to Him in prayer. He is waiting for you with outstretched hands - don't just reach to hold on - climb right in and let Him cradle you in the palm of His hand. Put all your trust in God and always rest assured that He has the perfect plan for your life! There is an old hymn that I love, "Tis So Sweet to Trust in Jesus." It is - isn't it?!

   The patchwork of my life is still in progress and I really do not know what the remaining blocks of my quilt will be like but I do know the Primary color will remain the same and the Thread that holds it together will grow stronger each day. It is refreshing to know that though the physical body grows old our souls remain young. We can take heart in that, but I must remember to keep them in sync - sometimes my soul gets so joyful I want to kick up my heels and dance but when I succumb to the urge my not-so-limber hip pulls me back to reality. Oh well, I have had my won-derful days of dancing, jumping and running and I treasure the memories. I think back to when I was the age Grandma was when she wrote her diaries. After school I couldn't wait to get out of my dress and into my jeans so I could run to the top of our hill. Exhausted I would lie down on my back in the hay field and look up at the blue sky and talk to Jesus - it was a special time and place for me to be alone with Him and share my day, my hopes and my dreams, and I prayed as she did that I could do some good in the world and be of some use to my God. Aspirations are high when you are young and I was so glad to read, when I was in my sixties, that Grandma felt as I did when we were girls. We always had a special bond but after I read her innermost thoughts, I realized that we were kindred spirits - our heart and soul love for God made our bonding even more secure.

72nd birthday with a few of my blessings

But life goes on and even though I am not as limber as I once was I find that I am more excited to be exactly where I am now with that stock pile of experiences to look back on and the pure joy of living today with its unexpected pleasures. Bruce called very early this morning - just to tell us he loved us - you think that doesn't make a day richer? Tom came over last evening to see how we were doing and to tell us about his day. We spent the afternoon with Sue and the children yesterday and Mark and Rebecca are taking us out to dinner tonight (with the children, of course). How much richer can we get? I will tell you. These lives - Gene's, mine, each child, each spouse, each grandchild, each great grandchild, knows Christ. That is as good as it gets. That is riches!

The seeds are ordered, the garden will soon be ready to plant, the rose-breasted grosbeaks, indigo buntings and goldfinches will return when the daffodils are in bloom. The lilacs will perfume the air and then the lupines will be a sea of color after the planted garden sprouts green to define each row. There will be family picnics and campfires, children's laughter and peaceful quietness.

Some year to come my children will put the binding on my quilt. I pray that as they work on it our Heavenly Father will be binding them together in even closer unity to protect, encourage and stand by each other and may the peace that passes all understanding be theirs forever and ever. Why does God put a humorous thought in my head even as I write something serious like this? In the days when we lived in Virginia Beach and Sue was four, five and six, television had a number of technical problems. Whenever the glitches happened they printed "PLEASE STAND BY" on the screen. As a dutiful mother I read it to Mark and Sue. When I did Sue would run to the set and stand by it straight as an arrow, until the problem was solved and the regular programming was back on the air. She didn't do it to be funny - it was just an example of her sweet and innocent obedience. Oh, that we all could run to "stand by" Jesus when He calls us in so many different ways each day and follow Him with sweet and innocent obedience!

My heart is full because He has given me peace. He has taught me to count everything for joy. He fills my heart with love. He lifts my burdens and shares my innermost thoughts. He hears my constant prayer and I know He really cares. He causes my heart to sing when I see Gene walk across the yard and He keeps our love fresh and beautiful. He fills me with hope for the future. He has taught me patience. He brings tears to my eyes when I grow thankful for our children and their children. He pours His blessings freely and He loves even me. - But best of all - He made it possible for Gene to come home for lunch!

I love you Jesus ! ! !
II Peter 1: 1-11

231

The end.

To God be the glory!